Wh
to Mind Your
Own Business

Every year, millions of students in the United States and around the world graduate from high school and college. Commencement speakers—often distilling the hopes of parents and four years of messaging from educators—tell graduates that they must do something grand, ambitious, or far-reaching. Change the world. Disrupt the status quo. Every problem in the world is your problem, awaiting your solutions.

This book is an antidote to that advice. It provides a clear-eyed assessment of three types of people who tend to believe and promote a commencement speaker's view of the world: the *moralizer*, who imposes unnecessary social costs by inappropriately enforcing morality; the *busybody*, who thinks the stranger and close friend merit equal shares of our benevolent attention; and the *pure hearted*, who equates acting with good intentions with just outcomes. The book also provides a bold defense of living an ordinary life by putting down roots, creating a good home, and living in solitude. A quiet, peaceful life can be generous and noble. It's OK to mind your own business.

Justin Tosi is Associate Professor of Philosophy at Texas Tech University. With Brandon Warmke, he is the author of *Grandstanding: The Use and Abuse of Moral Talk* (Oxford University Press, 2020).

Brandon Warmke is Associate Professor of Philosophy at Bowling Green State University. With Justin Tosi, he is the author of *Grandstanding: The Use and Abuse of Moral Talk* (Oxford University Press, 2020).

Why It's OK: The Ethics and Aesthetics of How We Live

ABOUT THE SERIES:

Philosophers often build cogent arguments for unpopular positions. Recent examples include cases against marriage and pregnancy, for treating animals as our equals, and dismissing some popular art as aesthetically inferior. What philosophers have done less often is to offer compelling arguments for widespread and established human behavior, like getting married, having children, eating animals, and going to the movies. But if one role for philosophy is to help us reflect on our lives and build sound justifications for our beliefs and actions, it seems odd that philosophers would neglect arguments for the lifestyles most people—including many philosophers—actually lead. Unfortunately, philosophers' inattention to normalcy has meant that the ways of life that define our modern societies have gone largely without defense, even as whole literatures have emerged to condemn them.

Why It's OK: The Ethics and Aesthetics of How We Live seeks to remedy that. It's a series of books that provides accessible, sound, and often new and creative arguments for widespread ethical and aesthetic values. Made up of short volumes that assume no previous knowledge of philosophy from the reader, the series recognizes that philosophy is just as important for understanding what we already believe as it is for criticizing the status quo. The series isn't meant to make us complacent about what we value; rather, it helps and challenges us to think more deeply about the values that give our daily lives meaning.

Titles in Series:

Why It's OK to Mind Your Own Business

Why It's OK to Mind Your Own Business

For further information about this series, please visit: www.routledge.com/Why-Its-OK/book-series/WIOK

JUSTIN TOSI AND
BRANDON WARMKE

Why It's OK
to Mind Your
Own Business

Routledge
Taylor & Francis Group
NEW YORK AND LONDON

Designed cover image: Andy Goodman. © Taylor & Francis.

First published 2024
by Routledge
605 Third Avenue, New York, NY 10158

and by Routledge
4 Park Square, Milton Park, Abingdon, Oxon, OX14 4RN

Routledge is an imprint of the Taylor & Francis Group, an informa business

ISBN: 978-0-367-14173-8 (hbk)
ISBN: 978-0-367-14174-5 (pbk)
ISBN: 978-1-003-45924-8 (ebk)

DOI: 10.4324/9781003459248

Typeset in Joanna and Din
by codeMantra

For our students

Contents

Acknowledgment

We are fortunate to have so many people to thank for their help in making this book far better than it otherwise might have been. We are grateful to the Institute for Humane Studies for a research support grant and a book manuscript workshop they hosted in November 2020. Jason Brennan, Jessica Flanigan, Christopher Freiman, Bradley Jackson, J.P. Messina, Rebecca Tuvel, and Bas van der Vossen read an early version of the book and gave us excellent comments during that event. We are indebted to two careful and thorough referees for Routledge whose comments helped us tremendously. Brad Skow graciously read the entire manuscript and gave us wise feedback about how to deal with some tricky philosophical issues. We've benefitted from many conversations with Hrishikesh Joshi, David McPherson, Kevin Vallier, and Craig Warmke. Tradition and honesty compel us to acknowledge that all remaining errors and deficiencies are solely our responsibility.

We have discussed various parts of this book with audiences at the Philosophy, Politics, and Economics Society, Georgetown University, West Virginia University, and the University of Minnesota, Morris. Audiences there asked many great questions that helped us see how to improve the book.

Our graduate students helped us see our way through some of these issues, specifically during Justin's graduate seminar on social morality at Texas Tech University in spring 2019, and Brandon's graduate seminar on social morality at Bowling Green State University in fall 2020.

We're very grateful to Routledge for believing in this book, and especially to our editor Andy Beck and his assistant Marc Stratton for being so supportive and patient.

Special thanks are due to our department chairs, Mark Webb and Joel Velasco at Texas Tech, and Michael Weber at Bowling Green, for their support during our work on this project.

We thank our families for the roots and homes they provided us early in life.

We apologize to anyone we forgot.

Acknowledgment

There happen to be whole, large parts of adult American life that nobody talks about in commencement speeches.

David Foster Wallace, "This Is Water"

We are never more high-minded about what matters in life than when we are at commencement ceremonies. As new graduates prepare to head into the real world, speakers tell them to get out there and make their mark.

Michelle Obama gave this charge to Oberlin College graduates in 2015:

> Every city ordinance, every ballot measure, every law on the books in this country—that is your concern. What happens at every school-board meeting, every legislative session—that is your concern. Every elected official who represents you, from dog catcher all the way to President of the United States—they are your concern. …
>
> Make sure the folks who represent you share your values and aspirations. See, that is how you will rise above the noise and shape the revolutions of your time. That is how you will have a meaningful journey on those clamorous highways of life.[1]

DOI: 10.4324/9781003459248-1

Speeches like this are common. That same year, science popularizer Bill Nye told Rutgers graduates to "Become the next Great Generation! You can and you will—dare I say it, Change the World!"[2] Television host Katie Couric counseled students to make a big splash: "You got to get out there and get yourself noticed."[3] Novelist Salman Rushdie admonished Emory grads not just to change the world, but to reinvent it. "Try not to be small. Try to be larger than life. … Make no mistake. You can change things. Don't believe anyone who tells you that you can't. … Reinvent the world."[4]

Commencement addresses celebrate the admirable things that we do together on a large scale. They invite young adults to do their part in addressing big social problems. These speeches are invariably uplifting and almost exclusively positive. You can't fault young people for walking away thinking the way to have a meaningful life is to scour the planet for problems, solve them in grand style, and get yourself noticed.

Rare is the commencement speaker who warns bright-eyed graduates about the downsides of reinventing the world, getting involved in others' affairs, and surveying the moral landscape for problems to fix. A celebrity who tells graduates to settle down and tend to their own affairs will make university administrators wonder whether they wasted a lot of money. (Public universities not infrequently pay commencement speakers upwards of $100,000 for a 20 minute speech.[5])

Commencement speeches hold up as moral exemplars those who set their minds on reinventing the world and solving others' problems. Graduates are told those with meaningful lives shape the revolutions of their time, leaving the rest of us to wonder whether we are wasting ours. Those behind the podium may not explicitly condemn those who choose to mind their own business and focus on their own problems, but you don't have to look hard to find that message expressed in our culture, too.

Take, for example, Charles Dickens's beloved *A Christmas Carol*. Early in the story, charity collectors ask the miserly Ebenezer Scrooge for a donation to the "poor and destitute." Scrooge rejects their pleas, snapping "It's enough for a man to understand his own business, and not to interfere with other people's. Mine occupies me constantly."[6] Few readers think Scrooge has the right moral outlook here.[7] Only selfish people mind their own business.

Later in the story, Scrooge is visited by his deceased but ghostly business partner, Jacob Marley, who has returned to tell a tale of regret. Though in life Marley shared Scrooge's commitment to minding his own business, in death he has realized his mistake. "Mankind was my business," Marley cries. "The common welfare was my business; charity, mercy, forbearance, and benevolence, were, all, my business. The dealings of my trade were but a drop of water in the comprehensive ocean of my business!"[8] For postmortem Marley, minding your own business is just an excuse for selfishly shirking your social responsibilities.

Sometimes the idea of minding your own business is associated with another frequently maligned approach to life: political disengagement. Disapproval of those who tend to their own affairs and stay out of politics dates back to ancient times. In his *History of the Peloponnesian War*, Athenian general Thucydides recounts a funeral oration given by the eminent politician Pericles. In what has become a classic statement of Western democratic ideals, Pericles declares "we do not say that a man who has no interest in politics minds his own business, we say he has no business here at all."[9] Just keeping your head down and doing the best you can for your friends and family is not enough in a democratic society, where everyone's business—every school-board meeting, every legislative session—is your business.

More than two thousand years later, minding your own business about social and political matters is still held in contempt. In Sinclair Lewis's 1937 novel *It Can't Happen Here*, the United States elects as president Berzelius Windrip, a populist strongman who gradually imposes authoritarian rule. In the immediate aftermath of Windrip's election, the protagonist Doremus Jessup wonders whether it's okay to live a quiet life and mind his own business:

> Is it just possible … that the most vigorous and boldest idealists have been the worst enemies of human progress instead of its greatest creators? Possible that plain men with the humble trait of minding their own business will rank higher in the heavenly hierarchy than all the plumed souls who have shoved their way in among the masses and insisted on saving them?[10]

As the story unfolds, however, Jessup comes to abhor these thoughts. The lesson of the novel, foreshadowed in these lines, is that good people like Jessup cannot simply mind their own business when faced with the Windrips of the world, or any other political problems for that matter. We must be vigorous and bold advocates for the good. We might fail in our mission, but we have to try.

The moral lessons offered by so many commencement speakers are common and enduring themes in our culture. There's a good reason for that. These are inspiring messages that are, up to a point, hard to disagree with. Is there anything more understandable than wanting to make the world a better place? Who would argue that we should just stand by and watch while a tyrant consolidates his power? Why shouldn't the most advantaged members of society do their best to help the least advantaged? Aren't we all required to root out injustice where we find it?

According to Commencement Speech Morality, a morally good life is one of acting out your good intentions to make big changes in the world. People find this outlook appealing for a reason.

But it's not an accident that most people—even those who are especially moved by such sentiments—seem to forget the lessons of Commencement Speech Morality quickly after encountering them. For all the messaging about solving social problems and changing the world, many of us live quiet lives and devote our energies to our families, friends, immediate communities—and even ourselves.

You might think people turn their backs on Commencement Speech Morality because they are weak-willed. They believe they should abandon their ordinary lives to help others, but they just can't bring themselves to do it. Or perhaps you suspect that most people are just selfish and have no qualms about ignoring the pressing moral issues of their time. But we think there's a better explanation for why people turn their backs on Commencement Speech Morality.

Nineteenth-century British philosopher John Stuart Mill sometimes referred to thinkers he admired but disagreed with as "one-eyed men."[11] Mill's one-eyed men saw part of the truth with stunning clarity and worked out impressive theories based on what they saw with single-minded devotion. But they did so at the expense of missing most of the truth. This is the mistake of Commencement Speech Morality. The view from the podium is limited. Even though it succeeds in identifying something important, it misses most of what matters from the moral point of view. The problem isn't that we're too weak-willed or selfish to do the right thing. Instead, the problem is that Commencement Speech Morality is wrong about what it means to live a morally good life.

This book sees the world from an alternative perspective, which we'll call Ordinary Morality, a view, not from the podium, but from the local library, the kitchen table, the backyard garden. Ordinary Morality is, we believe, the way most people understand what it means to live a morally good life after graduation weekend is over and real life once again comes calling. It isn't that we forget about what sounded so important in the moments we were inspired to care deeply about solving the world's problems. Rather, our moral vision expands, and we see that many other worthwhile values compete for our time and attention. We get an exciting opportunity at work to challenge ourselves and achieve something we care about. Our children ask us to read an extra bedtime story. We find a topic about which we want to acquire lots of interesting knowledge. And sometimes we just like to do things for fun that don't help anyone else or even engage any of our higher talents. When we're faced with options like these, minding our own business sounds pretty good. And that's because it very often is.

According to Ordinary Morality, a morally good life isn't just about changing the world and shaping the revolutions of our time. Instead, it's about choosing well from among the many things that are worth doing. Sometimes morality really does require doing your part to solve big problems that affect the whole world, like contributing to relief efforts for the victims of an earthquake. But frequently there are smaller-scale projects close to home that are worth choosing, too.

For instance, instead of spending your Saturday collecting donations for UNICEF, it might be a morally worthy alternative to mow an elderly neighbor's lawn or help out at your children's school. It's also perfectly respectable to spend that Saturday doing things that enrich your own life. You matter, too. If your life is so thoroughly devoted to minding others' business that you end up neglecting your own, you're letting yourself and the people close to you down. Ordinary Morality recognizes that it's not only OK to mind your own business, it's morally important.

Commencement Speech Morality has an obvious reply. Sure, you make the world a better place by helping people in your community, and even by having fun doing your own thing. But with the time and resources you devoted to those things, you could have done *even more good* by instead giving to a highly effective charity. After all, rather than minding your own business, you could have picked up an extra shift at work and donated those wages to Malaria Consortium. According to GiveWell, an organization that assesses the cost-effectiveness of charities, it costs $6.80 to provide one person in Africa or Southeast Asia with seasonal malaria chemoprevention.[12] However much good you do by minding your own business, you could probably do a lot more by taking on even a very small part of the larger world's problems.[13]

Ordinary Morality disputes the simple claim that giving to a charity like Malaria Consortium does *more good* than the things you might do closer to home. This isn't to deny the importance of taking on big problems like malaria in developing countries. Instead, the disagreement here is about how we can compare the importance of different things that are valuable. According to Ordinary Morality, it's a mistake to treat things like helping yourself or your family as just another case of helping people. When you do something good for your community, your family, or yourself, you promote different kinds of moral value. There is no simple way to compare the moral importance of teaching your child to read with the moral importance of preventing malaria infections in Africa. Different values are at stake in each activity. You can't compensate for letting your child down by doing more good for the global poor.

If you've read about ethics before, you might see some similarities between what we're calling Commencement Speech Morality and a well-known moral theory: utilitarianism. According to utilitarianism, the right action in any situation is the one that best promotes happiness.[14] Utilitarianism does share some features with our target, but that's just because it's one possible view among many that commits the error at the heart of Commencement Speech Morality. That error is in seeing morality as something simple. Sometimes this error takes the form of thinking morality is reducible to one simple principle. Other times it involves treating one moral value or principle as if it dominates all others. Commencement speakers and others who talk as if morality is just about solving the world's biggest problems aren't all utilitarians, but they are all guilty of oversimplifying morality.

Ordinary Morality doesn't see matters so simply. It recognizes that it's important to help people in general when you can. But it also appreciates the distinct importance of meeting your special obligations to those around you. And it also treats us as morally responsible for ourselves. We should develop our talents, acquire interesting knowledge, achieve worthy goals, and have at least a little fun. In short, Ordinary Morality endorses value pluralism. There are many valuable things in life, and all of them matter. There is no simple ranking of those values that provides a general template for a morally good life. Instead, the best we can do is consider what matters in our circumstances and try to choose wisely.[15]

At this point you might be thinking, what does it matter if people oversimplify morality? What's the big deal with people talking about the most demanding and selfless things we do as if those are the main things that matter morally? Most people don't need to be reminded to pursue their own interests, care for their families, or even help the people around them. All those things are associated with vivid rewards and incentives. It's enjoyable to go for a walk or see that you're helping someone close to you. But we could all use a reminder now and then that people greatly admire selfless devotion to projects with no immediate feel-good results. Paradoxically, the critic says, it's the most important stuff that needs to be boosted in our consciousness. Otherwise we'll follow our immediate inclinations and leave distant problems unaddressed.

Part of the problem with Commencement Speech Morality is that it distorts and diminishes the value of minding your own business. It treats helping your friends, family, and yourself as at best inefficient alternatives to addressing the world's bigger problems. That distortion is a serious shortcoming on its own. But there are other problems with simplifying morality in this way. If morality is so simple, and there is a clear hierarchy of moral priorities, then it is easy to figure out when people aren't doing the right thing. If you know someone isn't engaged in social activism aimed at addressing a problem that affects a lot of disadvantaged people, then you also know she isn't living a morally good life. There's no need to pause and consider that she might be doing important things close to home that don't make a big splash, because those things are relatively unimportant. Maybe she is no worse than a lot of other people, but that's only because they're not living morally good lives, either.

The point is that Commencement Speech Morality doesn't just make minding your own business seem like a way of ignoring the most important demands of morality. It also licenses people to become judgmental moralizers who interfere with those who *do* want to mind their own business. If your neighbors were good people, you'd see them at least once in a while at the protests and rallies that good people like you attend. Those who take such a simple view of what it means to live a morally good life might even go one step further and become moral busybodies. Surely your neighbors aren't *really* bad people. They just need your help: a little information and encouragement about where and how the real difference-makers are spending their time. How could anyone spend all Saturday on their kid's science fair project when they know they have the option to hand out pamphlets on a street corner instead? If morality is as simple as commencement speakers seem to think, then it's hard to understand why decent people don't do the right thing, and easy to justify judging and badgering them for it. Going even further, Commencement Speech Morality can lead us into simplistic activism, encouraging us to attack a host of complicated problems in far-flung parts of the globe while armed with little more than our good intentions.

This book is a defense of minding your own business. Thus, it's a corrective to the bad advice people so often give when they're thinking in simplistic terms about a morally good life. In the first half of the book, we'll explain the pitfalls of minding others' business, and explain why it's OK to stay out of other peoples' affairs. In the second half, we'll show that it's OK to mind your own. While there's no single way to mind one's business, we will argue that it's morally permissible—even morally admirable—to devote your time and energy to your local community, neighbors, and family. And although we don't think it's ideal for everyone—or even many people at all—we'll even defend the value of living a solitary life that has little impact on anyone else. The common thread that runs through all these chapters is a commitment to Ordinary Morality and particularly to value pluralism. Value pluralism is therefore our starting point, not our conclusion. Of course, not everyone who thinks and writes about ethics agrees with us about this. That's OK. But it's important to be upfront about our starting assumptions. We do hope, however, that most readers will find the moral outlook we present in this book compelling and attractive.

Although we take ourselves to be defending a view about morality that most people find appealing, we expect that some will bristle at the idea that minding your own business is a good thing. This book won't please everyone, but we'd rather those who are displeased react negatively to something it actually says, rather than what they imagine it says. To that end, here are a few things the book doesn't say. We don't think people should be selfish, and we don't argue that they should live however they please. We won't argue that people who try to do morally ambitious things, including activists, are all bad people. And we don't claim that minding your own business is such a strong moral requirement that it isn't sometimes overridden by other moral demands.

Many things in life are morally important. Minding your own business is one of them. In the rest of this book, we'll try to show that minding your own business is more important than you might expect.

The Moralizer

2

> At a dinner party, for instance, don't tell people the right
> way to eat, just eat the right way.
>
> Epictetus, Enchiridion 46

The first half of this book is about what can go wrong when we mind others' business rather than our own. This chapter presents the moralizer, an overzealous promoter of his moral beliefs, the more exacting the better. Chapter 3 concerns the busybody, who probably means well but oversteps boundaries in his eagerness to help others. And Chapter 4 covers those who confidently set out to solve complex problems armed with little more than good intentions. In each of these chapters we will show you the pitfalls of minding others' business. We demonstrate how things can go wrong when we treat morality as simple, straightforward, and in heavy tension with everyday concerns, rather than a complex set of broad considerations that must be weighed carefully. Once we consider the problems that minding others' business can cause, we can see more clearly that minding our own business is a morally attractive way to live.

WHAT IS MORALIZING?

Some people are pushy about their favored brand of cell phone, their workout plan, or their multi-level marketing

DOI: 10.4324/9781003459248-2

scheme. Moralizers are pushy about morality, and more specifically their own take on morality. The nature of moralizers makes it likely that you have come across one, whether on social media, in a class, or at Thanksgiving dinner. They are always ready with a sanctimonious comment about whatever person, event, or policy is in the news. Few (if any) can measure up to the moralizer's lofty standards. The moralizer himself is not exempt from judgment, though he often hastens to add that he is engaged in constant self-examination and efforts to better himself—which he then points out is more than can be said for most others. Self-righteousness makes some people uncomfortable, but not the moralizer. He works hard at his virtue—or at least likes the idea of working hard at it—so why shouldn't others get to admire his achievement? They could stand to learn a thing or two.

People use the term "moralizing" in different ways. In perhaps the broadest usage, "to moralize" just means to apply moral considerations—notions of moral right and wrong, good and bad, virtue and vice—to a situation, thing, or person. This kind of moralizing—call it Broad Moralizing—just involves invoking or applying morality. For example, some people moralize in this way about art. In a conversation about a movie, your friend tells you about the tight script and the lighting, but then adds that the themes of the film are morally dark and that the supposed hero is actually a bad role model for kids. Your friend has simply introduced morality into thought or conversation. No problem.

On its face, there is nothing bad about Broad Moralizing. But often when we say someone is "moralizing," we mean to suggest they're making a mistake, or even doing something morally wrong. For this reason, some philosophers have suggested another sense of the term. We moralize in this sense when we make demands on others that introduce "illicit" moral considerations.[1] In other words, on this view moralizing involves making some kind of error. The error may take different forms. Sometimes, it involves inflating moral considerations by, say, turning an activity that is morally admirable into something obligatory. A colleague who accuses you of not sufficiently helping the poor because you only donate 10 percent of your income to charity might be moralizing in this sense. Here, the moralizer takes a real moral consideration (the duty of charity) but inflates it out of proportion (by demanding you give more than is morally required).[2]

Another way to introduce moral considerations illicitly is by applying them where they don't belong. In these cases, moralizers turn non-moral issues into moral ones.[3] At a yard sale, you offer to pay $9 for a lamp instead of the advertised price of $10. Were the seller to respond by demanding an apology for trying to take advantage of her when she has kids to feed, this would be a case of illicit moralizing. The moralizer has taken a fair offer in a context of negotiation and turned it into a moral affront. Moralizers of this sort engage in a kind of moral alchemy. Instead of turning lead into gold, however, they turn non-moral elements into moral ones.

There is certainly something to these notions of moralizing. Whether as moral inflaters or moral alchemists, illicit moralizers are overly strict or exacting in the moral demands they make on others.

And yet this approach still treats moralizing as a very broad phenomenon. The problem is that people often make inflationary or alchemic mistakes in their application of morality that don't strike us as cases of moralizing. Suppose, for example, you mention to a close friend that you think it's morally obligatory to recycle paper, and that she should start doing so. If it turns out you're mistaken and in fact it's admirable but not morally obligatory to recycle paper, then you'd be moralizing by inflating moral considerations. Or suppose that moral nihilists are right, and there are no correct moral standards at all: nothing is morally good or bad, right or wrong. Then all of us are moralizing whenever we make moral demands on others because we are turning non-moral issues into moral ones.[4] Thus, if you told others that "Killing people for fun is wrong," you would be moralizing.

It's fine with us if people want to use "moralizing" to describe such a broad class of mistakes. Like we said, the term "moralizing" is used in many ways. But there is a different sense of moralizing we are concerned with here—one that's still illicit, but not fundamentally about imposing inaccurate or overly strict moral views on others.[5] To work our way toward the sense of moralizing we have in mind, let's think about some obvious examples.

Some moralizers are aggressive proselytizers for their preferred way of thinking about morality, pushing their views on others whether they are interested or not. Confrontational "campus preachers," who visit college campuses with obnoxious placards and inflammatory slogans that they use to hector passersby are an extreme case. But this kind of moralizing also comes in less distasteful forms. We mind it less, but the young woman who interrupts your family time at the ice cream shop to impress upon you how important it is to support responsible water management in Mali is also moralizing. So is your co-worker who ignores all social cues to make sure you hear about the seven-part documentary she is watching on factory farming. Moralizers are sometimes like the salesperson who refuses to stop pitching.

In other cases, people moralize not by trying to recruit from among the unwilling, but by publicly applying their personal—and sometimes highly idiosyncratic—moral standards to others. Here again campus preachers are a good illustration of the extreme case, as they like to scream at young couples walking past, calling them hell-bound fornicators. But there are more mundane cases, too. Think of the person who responds to a social media post about a local fundraiser by saying that there are obviously more worthy causes in the world that people should support instead of this trivial one. Or take the acquaintance who accuses you of "reifying heteronormativity" when you refer to the woman to whom he is married as his wife, rather than his partner.

One element common to all these cases is that the moralizers are, in one way or another, overstepping important boundaries when they demand that others live by their moral code. To moralize, then, is to exceed the proper limits of your role as an enforcer of morality.[6] One fruitful way of seeing that there are such limits is by thinking about social roles and the kinds of behavior appropriate to them.[7]

Clergy preach moral lessons to their congregants. Doctors sometimes deliver moralistic lectures to their patients about taking better care of themselves for the sake of their loved ones. In many forms of therapy, on the other hand, part of the professional manner of therapists is to abstain from moral judgment. Lawyers acting in their professional capacity generally avoid blaming their clients. Judges at sentencing in criminal cases do not. The point is that whether we ought to press our moral views upon others depends upon our roles relative to those others.

Moralizers are less sensitive to the boundaries set by these roles than they ought to be. For moralizers, we are all justified in aggressively promoting morality, even if most people choose not to do so. We all have the capacity to form and critically examine our moral judgments, which we can then use to guide our actions. That same capacity licenses us to apply those judgments to other people by blaming them for their moral transgressions and persuading them to behave differently. Moralizers believe we all have the right to judge others in accordance with all of morality's requirements, and to act on those judgments. If other people refrain from pushing morality, that probably just means they lack the courage or integrity to do so, and it's up to moralizers to pick up the slack.

Moralizers are wrong. It isn't appropriate for just anyone to push their moral views on others indiscriminately, or to publicly blame people for their moral failings. It's one thing for your doctor to tell you to clean up your diet. It's another thing altogether for a stranger on the bus to give you the same lecture—even if he's a doctor.

Here's another way of seeing how moralizing oversteps boundaries. There are many kinds of moral requirements. Some of them concern clear and important interests of people in general. One such requirement is that we should refrain from killing other people without a good reason, like self-defense. For moral requirements like the duty against arbitrary killing, we all have good reason to express indignation when people violate them, to talk about how bad such violations are, and so on. But not all moral requirements are like that. In many cases, there are good reasons to refrain from enforcing our moral judgments, and when people do so anyway, they engage in moralizing. There are several ways your right to enforce your understanding of morality on others can be limited. Let's explore a few of those considerations now.[8]

Sometimes even when behavior is immoral, it isn't that important. For example, you might overhear a colleague lying to his wife on the phone, telling her he has to stay late at the office to grade papers, when in fact he just wants a few quiet hours to himself. Even if you know enough to be sure that he's lying and just wants to avoid another night of helping put the kids to bed, his transgression doesn't rise to the level of justifying intervention. You may have the capacity to recognize that his behavior is wrong, but that doesn't license you to tattle to his wife or scold him about how important it is to be honest with her. We can agree that his behavior is morally wrong, but it just isn't that big a deal as far as you're concerned. If you were to intervene in such a case, you would be moralizing. The relative seriousness of a wrong, then, is one way we can be limited in enforcing morality on others.

In other cases, people must make a decision and it's not at all clear what the right thing to do is. Perhaps competing values are at stake, and it's hard to see which is more important in the circumstances. Or maybe the situation is just really complicated, and it's difficult to acquire and weigh all the relevant information. There might be a fact of the matter about what a person should do, morally speaking, but it's difficult to see what that is. Moreover, the right thing to do might depend in part on nuanced considerations about the relationships involved, or about the choosing agent herself. For example, suppose a mother agrees to buy her son a video game for his birthday. Before agreeing, she did her due diligence. She read reviews about the game and paid special attention to warnings about its content. But as she goes to buy it, she discovers that the game is slightly more violent than the reviews indicated, and in her judgment, it is a bit much for a child her son's age. On the other hand, she has promised the game to him, and refusing to deliver on that promise now would damage the trust he puts in her. If you were to scold this woman for deciding either way, that would be moralizing. In cases like this one, where it is so difficult even for the people closest to the problem to figure out what's right, it would be inappropriate for others to impose their own moral assessment or blame people for failing to live by their own personal standards. Moral complexity and our often-blurry moral vision limit when we are justified in imposing our views on others. To intervene anyway would be to moralize.

Another way our right to enforce morality can be limited is due to a lack of standing. Generally speaking, we lack standing to instruct another person on the right thing to do or to enforce morality by expressing blame toward a wrongdoer when there is some fact about us that renders these kinds of behaviors morally inappropriate.[9] What kinds of facts? For one, people can lack standing because they're hypocrites. Think of a chain-smoker who has no intention of giving up his bad habit. Were he to lecture people about the harm they're doing to themselves and others by smoking, he would be moralizing. Second, as we hinted at earlier, people can lack standing because they don't have the right kind of social relationship with the person they're trying to correct. For example, spouses have standing to blame one another for failing to do a fair share of household chores. But it would be inappropriate for their bosses, neighbors, or mail carrier to issue similar expressions of blame. That's because none of those people have standing to intervene in this dispute between intimates. In this case, their moralizing would consist in enforcing morality outside the limits set by their social role.

A final limit on our right to enforce morality arises from the possibility that there are some aspects of morality that no one has a right to enforce at all. Consider what W. D. Ross calls duties of self-improvement.[10] These are duties to promote our own good, develop our talents, and in short to make something of our lives. Suppose that instead of spending his free time reading Dostoyevsky and Shakespeare and developing meaningful relationships, Tosi retreats to a private life of gluttony, sloth, and self-abuse. It would certainly be fitting if he felt some self-reproach. He would be wasting his life and letting himself down. But this might be an aspect of morality that no one else (or at least no one else beyond his closest friend and co-author) has a right to enforce. Most everyone lacks the right to tell us we shouldn't waste our own time. When people socially enforce these more private aspects of morality anyway, they moralize.

We've tried to identify some limits on our right to enforce morality. But we haven't sought to give an exhaustive list of those limits. And it's OK if you don't agree with us about all of them. Furthermore, we are sensitive to the possibility that these limits differ somewhat across cultures. What is important to see is that we don't always have a right to enforce morality. To put it in philosopher's terms, not all morality is social morality. In fact, we think the default is that morality should not be enforced, and the burden of justification is on those who want to enforce it. As many of our examples illustrate, our right to enforce morality will often have to do with our social role. In sum, then, you can think of moralizing not as applying morality where it doesn't belong, but applying it where you—as its enforcer—don't belong. You might be right that a mother shouldn't have bought a violent video game for her son, or that someone isn't making the most of his life. But just because your moral judgment is accurate, that alone doesn't license you to do something about it. Sometimes that's because it's not your place for one reason or another. Other times it's no one's place at all, because some parts of morality should not be socially enforced.

THE COSTS OF MORAL INTERVENTION

Some readers might be puzzled by our notion of moralizing. How could there be anything morally objectionable about discouraging others' immoral behavior? Sure, there might be good reasons not to intervene when you see someone doing something wrong. You might worry about a confrontation turning violent, for instance. Or you might just feel uncomfortable confronting people, even when they're wrong and you're right. But, the thinking goes, you would not be making any kind of moral mistake simply by enforcing morality. Thus, your authors must have made some kind of mistake in our account of moralizing if we think it is morally objectionable. In fact, when we've talked about moralizing with audiences, we are commonly asked, "So what? What's the big deal about trying to get people to do the right thing, or to stop committing wrongs? Isn't this all a bit precious?"

We understand why some people, including many moral philosophers, think like this. But in our view, this way of thinking is a mistake. We can even pinpoint the most likely source of error. Once you understand the nature of this error, much of what is unhealthy about our social practices of enforcing morality will make a lot more sense to you. Unfortunately, you'll also see the problem everywhere.

We can all agree that morality is important. If we lived in a more just society, people would generally be better off. It is appropriate to want our actual, non-ideal world to be more just, and it is worthwhile to try to make it so. But it is also crucial to recognize that our interventions to make the world morally better are costly. Moralizers do not, and that is the heart of the problem.

In this context, we can understand a cost to mean something that's suffered, a burden that people have to bear. The costs of moral intervention come in many currencies. Familiar ones include the emotional "sting" of being publicly blamed or morally lectured, the interruption to what people were doing, their time spent listening to your correction or explanation, the risks of them responding in kind with their own blame and moral lecturing, the damage to relationships, and most significantly, the coercion you apply by intervening as you do. These costs aren't always high. They're also frequently outweighed by the benefits of moral intervention. But it is important to recognize that they exist. Moral enforcement isn't free just because it's often worth it.

To see this, let's consider an example of minor immoral behavior, which we suspect most readers will agree should be left alone. Suppose you see a mother and her young daughter at the grocery store. The mother is clearly exhausted and trying to get through her shopping as quickly and quietly as possible, but her daughter keeps pestering her about buying a different cereal. Finally, the mother snaps and issues an inappropriately stern rebuke to her child, who is obviously hurt and embarrassed by the outburst. The mother's behavior is wrong. People should be kind to each other, and parents have even stronger obligations to be kind to their children. But it would also be wrong for a stranger to intervene to explain this to the mother, demand that she apologize to her daughter, or offer parenting tips about how she might have handled the situation better. Even in a simple example like this one you can imagine lots of reasons not to do any of these things—people could have violent outbursts, maybe this is out of character and the mother will apologize on her own later, etc. But we think the strongest reason not to intervene is that the cure is worse than the disease—the cost of intervening is not warranted by the degree of wrong done or the likely moral improvement that would come from addressing it.

Intervening in any of the ways mentioned would be an unjustified imposition.

This diagnosis suggests that when we enforce morality, we do something costly. By imposing our moral judgments on other people, we at least attempt to wield power over them, demanding their attention and pressuring them to behave as (we say) morality requires. This is true even when our moral judgments are correct, as in the case of the impatient mother.

To some readers this point probably seems so obvious that it's hard to see how anyone could disagree. But many moral philosophers do.[11] They think of morality as special in one way or another. When we make moral claims on one another, there is nothing personal about it, on their view. The claims we press on other people when we intervene to promote morality have a special status that other interpersonal demands lack. Pressuring someone to do the right thing is not like trying to get them to watch your favorite TV show, water your plants while you're out of town, or to do anything else you want them to do. The demands of morality aren't an imposition like those other things might be, says the critic. The morally right thing is what we should do anyway.

We need not explore the various accounts philosophers have developed to explain this supposedly special status of morality. For our purposes, it's enough to say that these views cannot make sense of examples like that of the impatient mother, where it seems obvious that moral intervention is costly, and costly in such a way that it's hard to see how the imposition is justified. We can agree that it would have been better if the mother had found a more gracious way to deal with her daughter's behavior, and that she acted badly by snapping at her. But making that appropriate judgment privately and acting on it are two importantly different things.

When we act on our moral judgments by blaming others or otherwise intervening in their affairs, we apply coercive social pressure.

Someone might object that our claim about moral intervention being costly might do a fine job of explaining our reaction to cases like that of the impatient mother, but it doesn't seem as plausible in others. More specifically, in cases where moral intervention seems very important and obviously justified, you might hesitate to say that intervention is costly coercion. To make things hard for ourselves, let's consider an extreme example. Suppose you see someone about to beat another person up, and you could easily intervene to stop the assault from happening. Let's even make it as easy as possible to do so—say you're a compelling speaker, and you know the would-be assailant to be impressionable. The right word or two from you about the moral worth of the person he's about to beat up would get him to back down.

Even in this case, our view says your moral intervention is costly. Some will balk at that result. But this application of the view seems correct to us, for two reasons. First, even if your intervention is coercive and therefore costly, the benefit of preventing an assault vastly outweighs that cost. The balance of costs and benefits accounts for the commonsense thought that intervention is clearly justified. Second, although some might think it's strange to regard even an intervention this minimal as costly, compare it to a case in which you don't intervene at all. It would have been better still if the would-be assailant had suddenly decided not to attack anyone, without any prompting from you or anyone else. But if an outcome that includes you doing nothing at all is better than the same outcome with your intervention, then intervention must carry some cost, even if it is morally justified.

We've focused here on arguing that moral intervention is costly because it is coercive. But additional factors beyond the degree of coercion could also contribute to the cost of an intervention. Sometimes intervention is more or less costly due to the role the intervener plays in that person's life. It's one thing for your wife to criticize you for not taking a more active role in your children's lives. It's quite another for your neighbor to do so. It's fine for a moral philosophy professor to deliver a lecture about the nature of the good life. Most would not be so tolerant if a flight attendant delivered a similar lecture after the in-flight safety instructions. It sometimes also matters whether the person being subjected to a moral intervention accepts the moral demands being issued. Warmke might reluctantly nod in agreement if a pastor admonished him to date only chaste women. Tosi would not respond so meekly. In other cases, acceptance doesn't seem to matter, like when we blame an unrepentant murderer for his crimes.

We can now see why it makes sense to think that our right to enforce morality is limited, often by our social roles: these limits help reduce the costs of moral enforcement. When we all recognize that our authority to act as the moral police is limited in various ways, we lower the risk that our moral enforcement will be pointless or oppressive.

To drive this point home, it's worth exploring in more detail some of the costs of moral intervention. So in the rest of the chapter, we'll discuss a few ways moralizing causes social problems. Each of these problems arises in part because moralizers don't recognize the costs of moral intervention.

Again, we won't offer an exhaustive list. Nor will we present any criteria for determining when the costs of moral intervention are worth it. The important thing to understand is that there are costs. Moral intervention doesn't occur on a frictionless plane. It comes at a price. If more people appreciated this point, there would be less moralizing. Moralizers either pay little heed to the costs they inflict on others by delivering their unwanted sanctimonious sermons, or they act as if there are no costs to their behavior at all. Moralizers are skilled at always finding some pretext to criticize others, so their failure to appreciate the downside of their morality habit leads them to be a constant annoyance for those unfortunate enough to be around them.

Inappropriate Demands

One of the things we find most troubling about moralizers is their tendency to subject other people to inappropriate moral demands. We don't mean that the moralizer merely has made a demand on others that involves a false moral claim, though that will often be the case, as we saw at the beginning of this chapter. Rather, we mean that moralizers are out of line just by making the demand.

To see this, consider that when someone publicly blames you, or tells you that you should live your life differently, they are attempting to wield a kind of authority over you. If other people are sympathetic to the idea that you're behaving immorally, you could lose your livelihood, important relationships, or even be completely ostracized. Moral demands are presented as authoritative, and to rebuff them puts you in conflict with the person issuing them. On the other hand, acceding to someone's moral demands seems to grant them the authority to direct your behavior. All of this is less troubling in the right circumstances, as we've said, but the fact remains that making and responding to moral demands is a delicate process. Moralizers do not handle it appropriately. Worse still, habitual moralizers go through life blithely peppering others with moral criticism or moral demands as it pleases them.

One reason that moralizers' demands on others are inappropriate is that, as we have already noted, they lack the standing to issue them. Moralizers believe that everyone has the morally sanctioned power to issue moral demands to anyone else. It doesn't matter who the demand comes from, only that it represents a genuine moral requirement. Moralizers, as Bernard Williams puts it, act "as if every member of the notional republic [of morality] were empowered to make a citizen's arrest."[12] We grant that some moral requirements should be enforceable by all—arguably those that protect people from serious and immediate harm, for instance. But this is not true of moral requirements in general. The mere fact that you have a moral judgment about someone's behavior does not license you to issue a demand based on that judgment, even if it's accurate. It isn't your place to intervene unilaterally in an argument between intimates to express your judgment about who is morally at fault. You shouldn't scold someone if you overhear him on the phone lying to his partner about where he currently is. You shouldn't criticize a stranger at a cafe for not ordering fair trade coffee. Notice the problem isn't just the *manner* of reproach. You lack standing even if you enforce your moral views quietly, pulling that customer aside and gently encouraging them to change their coffee buying habits.

As we've said, we don't have a general theory of what features of a situation grant someone standing to apply their moral judgments to others, though it will surely involve the norms that govern our relationships more generally.[13] We hope that most readers will agree that we do not have a general permission to police all aspects of others' behavior under the banner of enforcing morality. If that's correct, then one way moralizers impose inappropriate demands on others is doing so when they lack standing.

Another way moralizers make inappropriate demands is by treating non-universal moral requirements as universal ones. Moral values are expressed differently in different places, and this sometimes leads to disagreement about whether some particular bit of behavior is, for instance, respectful or kind. Here's an example. Philosopher Jeanette Bicknell reports a real-life case of a park volunteer in Toronto causing a scene by rushing to cover up a mother who was breastfeeding her baby in public, then, after the woman complained, escalating the incident into a feud by self-righteously posting about it on the park's website.[14] We don't know exactly what the volunteer was thinking, but it is reasonable to surmise that she thought it lewd or immodest for a woman to reveal her breast in public, even for the purpose of breastfeeding.

This seems to us like something that people with different sensibilities or cultural backgrounds can reasonably disagree about. They might agree about the importance of the underlying values—respecting others, behaving civilly in public—but disagree about whether the behavior in question is in keeping with those values. This is a good reason not to go around aggressively imposing your judgments about such cases on other people. They might just be from another culture where different norms apply, or there might not be settled norms in your community about the relevant behavior. There may be local moral norms or not, but surely there are no universal moral norms about what exactly counts as disrespectful or lewd when it comes to breastfeeding. (You might feel more strongly one way or another about breastfeeding in public, but nothing hinges on this particular case. Feel free to substitute another relevantly similar case.) The point is that because moralizers are more prone to issue moral demands to others, they are also more likely to behave as the park volunteer did, acting as if their moral judgments are universally applicable. They are thus more likely to overreach, and issue inappropriate moral demands based on their own idiosyncratic experience and background values.

Finally, moralizers make inappropriate demands on others by nitpicking their behavior and subjecting them to hectoring moral criticism. The inappropriateness might have to do with the fact that moralizers call people to the mat for petty things, such as where they met their significant other ("You met her at a bar—not at church?"). Or it might have to do with the sheer volume of their demands: every time she sees you, your neighbor reminds you there's never been a better time to donate to Oxfam. Because they find fault with others' behavior so frequently, and are so eager to express those judgments, moralizers can be galling to be around. The weight of their demands is suffocating.

It can be tempting to play fast and loose with the moral demands we make on others. This may be because we want others to think we are virtuous and have high moral standards.[15] Or perhaps we want to exercise control over them. Telling others how to live under the pretense of The Demands of Morality makes us feel powerful.[16] Or we may feel compelled by our clear and detailed vision of morality to force its dictates on others. Whatever their motivation for being so demanding, however, moralizers make everyone pay the price.

Philosopher Robert Fullinwider writes that "morality imposes a basic division of labour: it requires from us charity toward others and strictness with ourselves."[17] Moralizers recognize no such division. Because their personal expectations are not accessible to those they judge, they are bound to be disappointed in other peoples' behavior and worse, willing to say so. Of course, many moralizers do their best to bridge this gap by publicizing their moral judgments as widely as possible, but this is the wrong way of resolving the problem. They should instead exercise some humility about their moral judgments and stop moralizing.

Interference with Practical Discussions

As moral philosophers, we're often frustrated by the quality of public discussions about moral issues. There are many ways these discussions go wrong, but perhaps the most irritating occurs when people fail to recognize that an expert in a scientific field like climatology, economics, or medicine is smuggling in moral claims under the guise of their expertise. A common refrain when these experts trespass into moral terrain is that they're just saying we should follow the science.[18] Even those who accept their empirical claims but question their practical prescriptions are labeled science-deniers or denounced as scientifically illiterate.

As a result, some members of the public labor under the mistaken impression that scientific studies have proven moral conclusions, when they can in fact do no such thing. Knowing how the world works is indispensable for figuring out what we should do about practical problems like climate change or epidemics. But we also have to engage in moral reasoning about what to do once we understand how things work. Science alone can't tell us that.

Scientists will be quick to point out that the reverse also happens. They're right. Sometimes instead of letting these experts have their say, people listen only to moralizers who've just thought about how the world ought to be. Rather than look into complicated issues about how the world works or what institutional barriers there might be to realizing their moral vision, many moralizers cut right to the chase and tell us what justice demands. Often without empirical evidence, they claim that the things they hate are the cause of all the world's problems, and the things they morally approve of are the solution. Their inquiry into the way the world works is thus limited to what philosopher Robert Nozick cheekily calls normative sociology, "the study of what the causes of problems ought to be."[19]

The consequences of moralizing about practical problems can be just as disastrous as pretending that science settles moral questions. Rather than do their homework and read up about the complex nature of social problems, moralizers either draw hasty conclusions on the basis of cherry-picked evidence, or they dismiss empirical evidence bearing on practical concerns as irrelevant. One U.S. politician recently illustrated this way of thinking when she expressed her dismay that, "there's a lot of people more concerned about being precisely, factually, and semantically correct than about being morally right."[20]

To take just one example, consider calls to impose rent control. Rent control policies restrict the amount that landlords can charge tenants for housing, or the amount they can increase rent each year for tenants renewing a lease. The lack of affordable housing in many cities is a serious moral problem, and on the face of it, rent control policies address that problem. For moralizers of a certain stripe, these policies are the obvious solution. They insist that anyone who opposes rent control doesn't care about the interests of poor tenants.[21] Moralizers don't always make false assumptions about how the world works, but they do in this case. There is overwhelming agreement among economists that rent control laws are counterproductive. In a survey of over 400 U.S. economists, 93 percent agreed with the statement "a ceiling on rents reduces the quantity and quality of housing available."[22]

The issue isn't just that moralizers are wrong about rent control, or any number of other hopeful claims about how to solve the world's problems. It also isn't that moral considerations don't belong in conversations about these problems. Of course they do. But moralizers overstep their role as promoters of morality by treating their simple moral claims or slogans as if they settle the matter when things are more complicated. They promote morality too aggressively without paying attention to the facts on the ground. Consequently, moralizers often use morality as a premature conversation-stopper. In some contexts, simple moral claims are enough to settle an issue:

> "Should I cheat on my wife?"
> "No! Cheating on your spouse is wrong!"

But in other contexts, moralizers use this same strategy to foreclose discussion about more complicated issues:

> "Should I vote for this rent control policy?"
> "Yes! Affordable housing is a basic human right!"

The point is that moralizing tends to crowd out discussion of other considerations that are important for making good practical decisions. Even if affordable housing is a basic human right, the moralizer has already decided that rent control is the best way to provide it. It's hard to interject and explain that a policy won't work when people are convinced that anyone presenting such doubts is simply morally benighted, or acting in bad faith: "Oh, so you don't think the poor should have housing?" The moralizer sits at the table with the policy experts and social scientists but doesn't let anyone else speak.

This, we can now see, is another cost of moralizing: it often shuts down inquiry. In their haste to get everyone on board with their views about what we should do, moralizers too often end up making irresponsible recommendations that aren't properly scrutinized. By promoting morality too aggressively, moralizers interfere with conversations that could otherwise promote good decision making.

The Efficacy of Moral Claims

If you've ever kept house plants, you've probably killed a cactus. Cacti don't need more than a quarter cup of water every month. And yet, nurturing people that we are, we end up drowning them, their sunken, gray carcasses a testament to our excessive enthusiasm. Though cacti need water, we don't do any good by being aggressive with our watering.

Applying our moral views to the world works in a similar way. Moralizers seem to operate on the theory that the more effort they put behind promoting morality, the better the moral outcome will be. But this is a mistake. We don't automatically make the world better by being more aggressive about blaming others or lecturing them about what justice demands, any more than we automatically make a cactus grow with daily watering.

In fact, a better course of action is to exercise some restraint about how we promote morality. We are more likely to persuade people to improve their moral beliefs or do the right thing if we pick our battles rather than sound the alarm about every moral imperfection we think we see. Why think that vigorously presenting our moral beliefs makes them less socially effective? One reason is that if moralizers pester people too much about what morality requires of them, many will come to resent the intrusion. They might come to think of morality as too demanding, since their every action seems to be subject to second-guessing from moralizers. If people are told that everything they do is at the very least morally flawed, then moral criticism will eventually lose its sting. People will become cynical about morality, and less reluctant to risk moral disapproval since they are bound to suffer it no matter what they do. That might mean they stop listening to the handful of moralizing individuals they encounter, or if moralizing is widespread enough, they might develop such an attitude toward morality in general. As philosopher Julia Driver memorably puts it, moralizers are "like a broken air conditioner—constantly running, making a lot of noise, but helping nobody and indeed probably spouting a lot of hot air."[23]

Some might doubt that people could be so callous in response to serious moral advocacy. If people see injustice in the world and notice that others are outraged, so the objection goes, that reaction tends to be infectious. So perhaps we need not worry so much about cynicism. Our moral emotions make it hard to just turn away from moral problems.

We agree that expressing emotions like moral outrage can help spur moral concern, both in ourselves and in others. But our moral emotions are finite resources, too, and if we use them indiscriminately, they will lose their power. As we have argued elsewhere, if people either feel or are exposed to too much moral outrage, they will eventually suffer from outrage exhaustion.[24] That is, they will be less moved by the outrage of others, and will no longer feel outraged so readily themselves, even when the feeling is morally appropriate. The psychological mechanism behind this phenomenon is called habituation.[25] When people are exposed to a stimulus repeatedly, their emotional reaction to it and similar stimuli will be weaker in the future. Thus, if you recount an upsetting story to a friend, you and she might be very upset on the first telling, but less upset on retellings, perhaps eventually having practically no emotional response.

Moral outrage works similarly. Because we can become habituated to things that trigger our emotions, people who are constantly working themselves into a moral frenzy over the minor news of the day risk becoming less affected by injustice in the long run. Thus, expressing moral outrage about every moral imperfection in the world—as some moralizers do—is a poor strategy for moving others to become more moral. Doing so will eventually backfire, as people run out of cares to give.

Worse yet, there is evidence from social science experiments that venting your moral emotions can actually serve as a substitute for taking more direct action. Economists David Dickinson and David Masclet ran a study in which participants played a public goods game. Each person was given the option to contribute to a central pot of money, which was then multiplied and split among the group for a nice return on investment. In such games, the group does best when everyone puts all their money in the pot. But each player also has an incentive to free-ride on the efforts of others, holding back his own money while still receiving the fruits of others' contributions. In this particular study, players were given the option after the game to pay to "punish" (impose a cash penalty on) those who didn't contribute.

Here's the twist: some groups were first allowed to vent their anger at the free-riders. Interestingly, in games where venting was allowed, players spent less to punish free-riders than in games without venting.[26] The lesson for our purposes is that outrage can expend our energy as well as build it up. If we vent too much hot air in expressing our anger at injustice, we might not feel so motivated to do anything more morally productive about it.

It's tempting to look at the world's moral problems and think that considerations of cost should not factor into our response to them. But that would be a mistake. We have limited resources at every step of the way in promoting moral progress, and we should use them strategically. If we just throw everything we have at the first thing that comes to mind, we won't get our money's worth. Moralizers resist this advice at the peril of those who need their help.

CONCLUSION

We don't doubt that many moralizers mean well. On the face of it, telling people to be extreme advocates for their moral beliefs sounds like morally sound advice. After all, morality is important. But as we've argued in this chapter, moral ends often aren't well served by vigorous advocacy. This doesn't mean that moral activism is bad. But we should remember that each of us has a limited role to play in the social enforcement of morality. When we overstep those limits we moralize, and society as a whole is left paying the costs.

To do one's own business and not to be a busybody is justice
Plato, *Republic* 433a

HOW TO BE A BUSYBODY

In introducing the busybody, we could scarcely do better than
the ancient Greek philosopher Theophrastus. In addition to
succeeding Aristotle as head of the Peripatetic School and
authoring some important works on botany, Theophrastus
also wrote a book about various moral characters. Among the
30 characters he discusses there is "the Busybody":

> In the proffered services of the Busybody there is much
> of the affectation of kind heartedness and little efficient
> aid. When the execution of some project is in agitation
> he will undertake a part that greatly exceeds his ability.
> After a point in dispute has been settled to the satisfac-
> tion of all parties he starts up and insists on some trivial
> objection. … He interferes in a quarrel between parties of
> whom he knows nothing. He offers to be guide in a for-
> est and presently he is bewildered and obliged to confess
> that he is ignorant of the way. He will accost a general at
> the head of his troops and inquire when battle is to be

DOI: 10.4324/9781003459248-3

given or what orders he intends to issue for the next day. He is wont to give his father information of his mother's movements …. When his wife dies he inscribes on her monument not only her name and quality but those also of her husband, father, and mother, and adds, "All these were persons of extraordinary virtue." He cannot take an oath in court without informing the by-standers that it is not the first time his evidence has been called for.[1]

Like moralizers, busybodies have boundary issues. They stick their noses into other people's business. "The mind of the busybody," writes the Greek philosopher and historian Plutarch, "is at the same time in mansions of the rich, in hovels of the poor, in royal courts, and in bridal chambers of the newly-wed. He searches out everybody's business, that of strangers and that of rulers."[2]

But whereas the moralizer's primary mode is that of critic, judge, or preacher, the busybody is the helper, the problem-solver, the savior. The moralizer is content to identify problems in the world—real or imagined. As the moral watch-dog, their job is done when attention has been drawn to what's wrong in the world. Moralizing itself rarely extends beyond rebuke, correction, or blame. But this is the point at which the meddling busybody begins her work, latching onto problems and applying herself to fixing them.

It is not just any problems that the busybody latches onto, though. She specializes in the problems of others. We don't call people busybodies for trying to get their own houses in order. Rather, the busybody presumes a position of oversight into other people's affairs. This idea is found in ancient discussions of busybodies. One author in the Greek New Testament, for example, combines two words, *episkopê* (to oversee) and *ta allotria* (the affairs of others) when he condemns the "busy-body": the *allotriepiskopos*.[3]

It is worth pausing to see that the boundary between moralizing and the busybody's meddling is fuzzy in part because they so often go together. Here are some examples where it looks to us like things start out with some moralizing, then shade into meddling:

> "If you're really trying to be fair, that's not how to do it. Here's the right way …"

> "I saw your proposed list of speakers for the conference, and I don't think that list is going to work. I took the liberty of sending you an updated list that's more diverse. I strongly encourage you to use it."

> "Excuse me, I saw your son teasing his little sister at the playground. You weren't around so I just pulled him aside and explained that's not how we should treat people. I'm pretty good at getting kids to behave."

However, meddling need not involve vocal moral criticism. Some busybodies bypass overt blame and just set out to do their good work. They see a problem in the world and try to fix it. What is important to understand is that moralizing and meddling can come apart, theoretically and practically, even if many people who aren't minding their own business pass effortlessly between them.

We can now see a simple way to distinguish meddling from moralizing, even if they're closely related. Moralizing involves overstepping your limits as an enforcer of morality. It is an inappropriate exercise of moral criticism. In a similar manner, the busybody's meddling is an *inappropriate exercise of helping behavior*.[4] The moralizer has boundary issues when it comes to intervening to judge others. The busybody has boundary issues when it comes to intervening to help others.

The busybody doesn't just offer his aid to others, though. In fact, he often doesn't even *offer* it at all. Rather he presumes to be in a position of authority or oversight and imposes himself upon others and their problems. The busybody's behavior is therefore typically inappropriate because, like the moralizer, the busybody will lack standing to intervene in others' affairs. Busybodies don't stand in the right kind of social relationship to the people they are trying to help. Stoic philosopher Epictetus asks of the busybody,

> What have you to do with other people's business? Why who are you? Are you the bull of the herd, or the queen bee of the hive?[5]

Meddling can also be inappropriate because the busybody doesn't know enough about the people or the affairs he intends to oversee. In this regard, perhaps the primary moral failing of the busybody is overconfidence. You have probably had the experience of going about your business and encountering strangers dealing with problems like the ones Theophrastus describes at the beginning of the chapter. Many of us react to these situations by thinking, "I don't know enough about this situation to be of much help, and I'd probably just get in the way if I tried." Or you might worry, "If this person can't figure out what to do here on his own, there's no reason to think I can swoop in and do any better." To the busybody, these reactions are just excuses not to help people in need. He intervenes where the rest of us lack the courage or know-how to help.

The inappropriateness of meddling may have yet another source. Plutarch located the error in the busybody's excessive desire to learn about the troubles of others, and a consequent lack of self-control in restraining himself from acting on those desires.[6] Busybodies are too curious about other peoples' problems. They are nosy, on the lookout for signs that others could be helped. And when busybodies do uncover others' problems, they can't help themselves. They intervene. Plutarch's advice to busybodies is to relocate the target of their moral gaze: "Shift your curiosity from things without and turn it inwards," he counsels. "If you enjoy dealing with the recital of troubles, you have much occupation at home."[7]

Whatever renders busybody behavior inappropriate—lack of standing, overconfidence, excessive curiosity paired with a lack of self-control, or some other factor entirely—not all meddling is equally bad. For example, some meddling is worse because the busybody has less standing to intervene: it is worse for the stranger at the grocery to reproach your children than it is for your next-door neighbor. Some meddling is worse because the intervention is more damaging. You overhear a married couple at the park reciting their financial troubles. Butting into their conversation ("Hi, sorry, I couldn't help but overhear you're having some money problems …") to give them the name of your financial advisor would probably be less damaging than butting in and trying to help by convincing them to invest their life savings in a brand new, can't miss cryptocurrency company.

Like many things in life, meddling in others' affairs can be inappropriate even if it has some good consequences. If you pull aside the stranger's kid at the playground and lecture him on the finer points of kindness, you might alter his life course and set him on the straight and narrow. Even so, you would be doing something inappropriate. Meddling is always some form of inappropriate helping behavior. There is always something bad about it.

We've been using the term "meddling" to refer to the characteristic behavior of busybodies. You might think, though, that engaging in just a little bit of meddling behavior once in a while doesn't necessarily make you a *busybody*. That seems right to us. Just like the badness of meddling can be understood along a spectrum, so can the extent to which one is a busybody.

At one end of the spectrum are those who engage in rare or occasional "light" meddling. It still may be okay to describe such a person as a busybody. We might say something like "Don't be such a busybody" upon observing a single act of meddling. But we would not want to say that such a person therefore has a trait of being a busybody (just like telling a white lie doesn't necessarily make you a liar, a person with the trait of dishonesty).

In a more heavy-duty sense of "busybody," the term refers to someone who has a stable disposition, across a variety of situations, to engage in inappropriate helping behavior. He meddles at work, at home, on vacation, and does it often. Such a person is a habitual busybody. This is the kind of busybody we will focus on in this chapter.

At the even more extreme end of the busybody spectrum are those with a messiah complex. Not merely habitual meddlers, these people take things a step (or several steps) further. They see themselves as maximally caring, exceptionally knowledgeable, and uniquely positioned to save others. They think they know how best to solve anyone's problem and aren't shy about letting people know it. They are on a mission to save people, whether they've been asked to help or not. You'll often see these busybodies bragging about the lengths they go to help, and how exhausting and frustrating it is to do the little bit they can, hoping they could just do a little more.

Human beings generally like to think of ourselves in positive terms, and the busybody is no different. Thus, he probably doesn't think of himself as a busybody. More likely, he sees himself as an advocate, an activist, an ally, or simply someone who *cares*. From his perspective, that's exactly what he's doing when he decides not to mind his own business. "Better to do some good than to stay in my comfort zone and avoid stepping on anyone's toes," he might reason. "They can thank me later," he thinks when others bristle at his unsolicited advice.

Busybodies think they're doing good, and they might be right in some cases. Yet the term itself connotes something negative. In everyday conversation, we often use the term to discourage people from invading others' privacy—"don't be such a busybody!" Nobody advises others to be a busybody, or even a do-gooder, at least in those terms. So the existence of busybodies presents something of a puzzle. On the one hand, everyone understands that it's possible to be a busybody— someone who engages in inappropriate helping behavior. On the other hand, many people, including your authors, have meddled in others' affairs. Some people are habitual meddlers. Others even see themselves as a kind of savior. What explains this? Why would anyone insert himself into other peoples' affairs, eager to offer help that is often ineffective?

In the rest of this chapter, we will consider two kinds of answer to this question. Each makes it understandable why someone could end up being a busybody, while also making it clear why it's a bad way to be. First, someone might become a busybody because she holds moral beliefs that demand she get involved wherever she sees an opportunity to help another person. Second, and more troubling, someone might be a busybody out of a pathological need to help others. Of course, some people are busybodies for both reasons, but we can consider the cases separately and simply apply both sets of remarks to those unfortunate souls.

A MORAL DEFENSE OF BUSYBODIES?

Most people make minor sacrifices for the good of others. They volunteer with community aid organizations, help classmates with difficult course material, or even donate a little money to international charities. Every serious moral philosopher recognizes that we owe at least a minimal duty of charity to those less well-off than us. Busybodies go much further than this, though. They go through life on the lookout for situations in which they might lend a helping hand. But even though their behavior is different in kind, it could have the same motivational root as the more common acts of charity described. Let us explain how the same reasoning that leads people to help others at all can easily lead to the conclusion that we should help others a lot more.

If you're reading these words, you're probably among the most advantaged people ever to live, and not just because this book appeals to a high-class clientele. Sure, you might have problems that cause you significant stress. You might be in debt, have family conflict, or just worry more generally about your future. But if you are capable of reading a book like this one (not to mention having the leisure time to do so), you probably live a comfortable life. Compared to a lot of people, you have it good. You could sacrifice a lot and still live far better than most. So, if you could give up a little bit of your time or other resources to help someone else a great deal, why wouldn't you?

This same question is illustrated vividly in the following influential thought experiment from philosopher Peter Singer:

> if I am walking past a shallow pond and see a child drowning in it, I ought to wade in and pull the child out. This will mean getting my clothes muddy, but this is insignificant, while the death of the child would presumably be a very bad thing.[8]

Most people think Singer is clearly correct about this case. It would be monstrous to refuse to rescue the drowning child simply to keep your clothes clean. But this reasoning generalizes to cover a broad class of similar cases in which most of us do not hesitate to focus on our own wants and needs. We buy new clothes, go out to eat, give gifts to our well-off friends and family, drive scenic but fuel-inefficient routes to work, and spend time and money on countless other things instead of donating to save lives that are just as important as the child in the drowning case. So what's the difference between that behavior and refusing to ruin your clothes to save the drowning child? Nothing morally significant, says Singer.

In Singer's view, it is wrong for us to use resources on morally insignificant creature comforts when we could instead use those same resources to do much more good in the world. In fact, he argues that we are all morally obligated to reduce ourselves to subsistence living and give our excess wealth away if doing so will save lives. The logic of this position is simple. If we're spending money on things we don't need to survive instead of saving others, we're treating our trivial pleasures as more important than preventing the deaths of other people who feel pleasure and pain just like us. But that seems indefensible. Surely buying a new pair of shoes isn't more important than saving someone's life. So, instead of spending so much of our money on entertainment, fine dining, or fancy clothes, we should be staying home in our studio apartments, eating (just enough) lentils, and giving our money to highly effective charities like Malaria Consortium.

Although it seems extreme, it's hard not to be sympathetic to Singer's argument. How can we justify spoiling ourselves with the finer things in life instead of saving lives? It's plausible that we don't respond to all the world's problems with the same urgency as we do the drowning child because it's much easier to ignore suffering when you don't have to stand there and watch. But as Singer and others are quick to point out, the mere fact that the drowning child is right in front of you and others are out of view, and perhaps far away, is a poor excuse not to treat them similarly. What matters is that in both cases, you could do something to save someone's life.

Many have been inspired by Singer's forceful and vivid arguments about the difference each of us can make. Some have dedicated themselves to lives of service, or taken stressful high-paying jobs only to donate most of their income to help the global poor. We'll have more to say about those who take on ambitious projects like this in the next chapter. Here we'll keep our focus on busybodies, who could be similarly inspired by reasoning like Singer's.

The strategy behind Singer's drowning child case is to present an opportunity to help someone right in front of you, and then argue that you should respond similarly in cases where you can help someone far away. The busybody might draw a different lesson from the case, though. The drowning child pulls on our heartstrings in a way that other people's problems rarely do. The plight of the drowning child concerns a good of great value. Here we have a situation where it's obvious that you should help. And the child will undoubtedly be grateful to be saved. And there doesn't seem to be any good reason to think you're a busybody for saving him: it doesn't appear that you lack standing, are overconfident, or have been too curious, for instance.

But sometimes you're in a situation unlike the pond case where you could still do a lot of good, even if intervening makes you a busybody. You might see a way to help someone who isn't so obviously in peril. Maybe the likely outcome for that person without your intervention isn't as dire as the loss of life, but you could still make a difference for them. It might not be as obvious what they need, and they might not even appreciate your help. But that doesn't mean you can't help. The busybody might then reason as follows: in the drowning child case we don't hesitate to help someone when it's easy, when we can help a ton, and when we're guaranteed a positive response to our behavior. But, the busybody continues, if we only help people in those ideal circumstances, we'll leave a lot of good undone. So, he concludes, we should be more willing to poke our noses into others' business, because what really matters morally is that we help people. If that means we run afoul of some antiquated social graces, then so be it. On the whole, it's morally worthwhile to be a "busybody." If you can help others, why *wouldn't* you?

We might help others by meddling in lots of ways. A busybody might engage in modest and relatively unobjectionable forms of unsolicited helping, like asking people who seem lost if they need help, pressing his preferred routes and shortcuts on them. Getting into more annoying behavior, a busybody might strut around the gym, looking for people whose deadlifting form he can correct. Or, eschewing more empty forms of small talk, he might give unsolicited diet advice to overweight strangers on the bus. We can imagine a busybody overhearing one side of a phone conversation and feeling emboldened to offer relationship advice. A busybody might have no compunctions about telling someone which politician it is in their self-interest to vote for. Taking the idea to the extreme, a busybody might sneak into her neighbor's house to water her plants or feed her pets. Or perhaps she could station herself by a pond and make sure everyone has a fishing license.

The point isn't that busybodies generally will do all or even any of these particular things. Rather, it is that the kind of busybody we have in mind goes through life looking for opportunities to make others' problems her own, on the theory that the morally right thing to do is to help whenever and however she can, and that it's better to help others than to help ourselves. It might seem plausible that morality requires us to do the sorts of things we've called meddling, at least if we can be judicious about it. We'll now argue that's a mistake.

EFFECTIVE BUSYBODIES AND THE WORLD'S WORST POOL PARTY

One of the most common responses to Singer's argument is that, in several ways, it is too demanding to claim we are morally obligated to respond to the distant needy in the same way that we would to the drowning child. We'll briefly describe these objections because they also apply to our attempt to extend his argument in defense of busybodies.

For one thing, critics say, Singer's position demands too much of us as we deliberate about what to do. To respond appropriately to all the cases of people in need, we would have to know a great deal about their situations. We'd also need to know whether the people or organizations to whom we might donate can actually help them, whether our donations would actually make a difference, and whether any cause would be more efficient to support than others.

These challenges are certainly less daunting now than in previous centuries, since our capacity for collecting and sharing information has improved so much. There are even effective altruist organizations that evaluate charities on precisely these grounds to simplify our deliberation about how best to do good. But it is still a lot to require people to think about and keep up with. And to be truly responsible, we'd also need to evaluate the methods used to compare charities.

Often this will involve considering questions of value that we cannot simply outsource to others. For instance, is it better to prevent a malaria infection, or to educate four children in East Africa for a year?[9] To consider all the relevant data along with these questions of value is probably more than most are capable of doing. So there may be no getting around the objection that the deliberation Singer asks of us is too demanding.

This objection carries over to the case of busybodies intervening in other people's affairs. Though here the problem is not only that there is too much to consider, but that busybodies by their very nature won't know everything they need to know. Busybodies undoubtedly think they know enough about the people they pester. But life is complicated, and except for those we know well, we often lack the knowledge of others' circumstances that is indispensable for giving reliably good advice. We don't know strangers' histories, or all the relevant facts about them, and we don't know what they care about in life. There aren't even any effective busybody organizations to offer guidance about how best to intervene. So even setting aside the fact that busybodies' interventions might be unwelcome, they will often be ineffective.

Consider the example of the busybody who tries to give relationship advice on the basis of overhearing one side of a phone conversation. He might think he recognizes a feature of the strangers' relationship that he has personal experience with, and that he can offer some gem of practical wisdom about it. It's not impossible that he's right. Some people have a Sherlock Holmes-level ability to pick up clues in such situations, and sometimes it's just obvious that it would make someone feel better to make a lighthearted remark, for instance. Our claim isn't that you should never try to help other people in situations like this one. Rather, it's that you shouldn't be eager to do so. Once again, it is a bad general approach to life to make everyone else's problems your own.

Now let's consider the second, and perhaps even more worrisome, demandingness objection to Singer. There are an awful lot of people in peril in the world. If he is right about what morality requires of us, then we really would be reduced to subsistence living if we tried to save them all. But that would mean that morality is extremely demanding. Living up to its dictates would require superhuman effort. But that can't be right. It might be difficult to be a good person all the time, but it shouldn't be next to impossible.

Perhaps some readers will think of the platitude "nobody's perfect," or the idea that we are all sinners by nature. But you can concur with those thoughts and still think Singer goes too far. For instance, on his view, if you pay one cent more for flavored lentils rather than choking down an unflavored alternative, you've done something wrong. Not something gravely wrong—it's only one cent—but it is a waste of a penny that could have been put toward saving someone's life before you selfishly wasted it. Surely this is absurd. Spending a few pennies, or even dollars, here and there to treat yourself does not make you morally blameworthy. You have a life, too, and it's OK to enjoy it.

Singer presents the drowning child case to represent a decision we make all the time—to pursue our own pleasure rather than save others' lives. But then he generalizes this decision to be about not just a single, isolated choice, but a whole approach to life. In other words, his moral advice is not to say, "just this once, do something to help someone else." Rather, it is to say, do nothing but help others and survive (so that you can continue to help others). To pinpoint what is going wrong with Singer's argument, we present another thought experiment, The World's Worst Pool Party.

> Suppose you find yourself at a pool party consisting of a deep pool, inattentive adults, and clumsy children. The adults are all deeply engaged in fun conversations, which you're free to join. The kids, who cannot swim, keep jumping in the pool anyway, and predictably need to be rescued as they start to drown. Nobody else reacts when a child starts drowning, so you jump in and save him. The pattern repeats itself a few times, and then you hear a few people making phone calls: "Bring your toddlers to the pool party and hang out with us. Don't worry, you don't have to do anything. There's a lifeguard." You spend all day at the party saving kids. You're tired, and you have to work tomorrow. But you know if you leave, people will die, and that is presumably a very bad thing.

Assuming you can't somehow break this party up, it is not at all obvious to us what you should do in this case. How many drowning children should you stick around to save? Do you have to stay until you'll die if you attempt one more rescue? That's too much, but it's the answer recommended by the principle that you should help others until it costs you something of equivalent moral value to what's at stake—your life, in this case.

The case of the drowning child involves a bait and switch. It doesn't address the question Singer is actually asking about what morality demands of us. The question isn't whether we should make a sacrifice to help someone just this once. It's whether we should sacrifice all the time and possessions we have, and will ever have, to help everyone in need. At some point it's OK to say you've saved enough drowning children, and it's time to attend to the rest of your life. It matters, too, as do the lives of people close to you: your parents, children, friends, and neighbors.

This demandingness objection is also applicable to the behavior of busybodies. We may not all be surrounded by drowning children, but if you look at people the way busybodies do, you'll see no shortage of people who could use your help. These people at the grocery store need to hear about how bad GMOs are. This guy is using the wrong kind of shampoo for his hair type. This internet acquaintance of yours seems sad, and he could probably benefit from rehashing what went wrong in his past several relationships for the next few hours. You could keep to yourself and avoid all these opportunities to help dozens of people a day in small ways, but they don't cease to exist just because you don't see them. Somebody somewhere needs change for a dollar, and you're going to find him.

True, the sacrifices of the busybody aren't as costly as those you might make by literally rescuing people all day at the world's worst pool party, but they add up. It's death by a thousand cuts. And the more people you actually succeed in helping, the more opportunities you're likely to find. Word of an endlessly patient and sympathetic ear spreads quickly, just as word of a free babysitter at a pool party might. If you try to help everyone for whom you could possibly make some small difference, you'll fritter away an awful lot of time and energy that you could spend more productively by minding your own business.

Time spent pursuing your own interests or helping people you're actually close to—real friends and family—is time well spent, as we'll argue in the second half of this book.

Taking care of yourself and the people you care about doesn't cease to matter from the moral point of view just because you enjoy it. Friendship is a morally significant good. And we owe it to ourselves to make the most of our lives, developing our talents and having fun where we can find it. These aren't values to be traded away when we can do slightly more good for strangers instead. They're things our lives are incomplete without. If you don't mind your own business, nobody else is going to do it for you.

On the other hand, maybe for some people there is no conflict between helping others and enjoying a life full of doing what you care about. These people might argue that helping others whenever they see an opportunity is just part of who they are, and they're good at it. They care about people in general in the way that most people care only about themselves and their loved ones. Like Marley's ghost, the well-being of all mankind is their business. They deny, in other words, that they've ever saved *enough* drowning children and it's time to tend to their own affairs. Helping others just is what they want to do. In these last two sections, we'll address two versions of the claim that minding your own business can include the pursuits of busybodies.

JOYFUL LIFEGUARDS?

Few would deny that people have a tendency to care more about those close to them. We care more about ourselves, our families, and friends than we do about distant strangers. But even if that is how most people feel, that doesn't necessarily mean they're right to feel that way. It also doesn't mean it's inevitable that people will take such a narrow view of who they care deeply about. Maybe we can grow out of the partiality to those close to us that appears to come so naturally. Then we won't be tempted to walk away when we've had enough of helping others. Rather, we'll all be joyful lifeguards, extending aid to the people we care about—everyone.

The ancient Stoic philosopher Hierocles proposes a simple but compelling way of thinking about individuals and our relationships with others. He wrote that we can think of ourselves as being at the center of many concentric circles. Each slightly larger circle includes people according to their increasing social distance from us, and therefore our degree of compassion for them. So, the circle immediately outside of ourselves is our closest family members. Then there is a circle for our extended family, and another for more distant blood relations. The layers of circles continue, with separate levels for the local community, residents of neighboring towns, co-nationals, and finally the entire human race. Hierocles argued that we should aim to draw all of these larger circles "closer" to us, so that we care about every other human being as we do family members, or even ourselves.[10]

Hierocles's circles of compassion have become a popular metaphor for describing ideal moral development.[11] The idea is appealing, up to a point. Extremely immature and selfish people care only about themselves, and maybe also some family and friends. Everyone else is either in the way or not their problem. According to some novels, at any rate, those who never leave their small towns are suspicious or disdainful of outsiders. And we have even heard tell that some care about the well-being of their fellow citizens, but not so much about the rest of the world. Part of becoming a mature adult involves developing a moral sense that recognizes the value of people outside your immediate circles. Perhaps our special concern for people close to us is also something we should grow out of. Why not think of everyone's business as your business, to be treated with the same degree of care?

We can imagine any number of mechanisms for spurring this expansion of our circles of compassion. We might rationally persuade people with moral arguments about the worth of every human life, or about the arbitrariness of someone being your neighbor rather than a resident of another country. There might be gradual cultural change, so that societies adopt more cosmopolitan values. We might introduce institutional reforms or create popular policies that help the least advantaged, and consequently people might gain a new appreciation for our shared fate as humans. Whatever the path, the point is that we should be hopeful for further development of our moral sense, and open to the idea that some people could care about everyone the way some care only about themselves. One hopeful interpretation of history is that more and more oppressed groups have gradually been recognized as deserving equal concern. Perhaps our circles of compassion can expand much further than most currently imagine.

We don't doubt that people can or should become kinder than they are or have been. Perhaps the more hard-hearted among us could care a bit more about people to whom we currently give little thought. But we doubt very much that living as a busybody, going through life jumping at every opportunity to help, is either feasible or good for anyone. When we try to extend our compassion to everyone, the result will not be expanding the circle of people we're moved to help. Rather, it will be that we get burnt out, no longer able to muster the effort to help anyone.[12]

Among people in caring professions—nurses, therapists, social workers—there is a phenomenon known as "compassion fatigue."[13] Compassion fatigue is a form of emotional exhaustion in which people become desensitized to tragedy and emotionally burnt out. Those suffering from it report feeling sad, inadequate, and exhausted. When people are in a state of compassion fatigue, they show less interest in upsetting issues, show muted emotional responses to them, and are less likely to seek out information about them.[14] Research suggests that people in caring professions develop compassion fatigue from repeated exposure to their clients' or patients' stress and trauma.[15] But there is also work suggesting that mass media can induce compassion fatigue among people more generally by way of their extensive coverage of upsetting news stories.[16] And some research suggests that even brief contact with someone suffering from psychological trauma can cause compassion fatigue.[17]

These results should be sobering for those who argue that we just need to care more about the whole of humanity so we can solve each other's problems. People who willingly enter caring professions are likely among those most sympathetic to that advice, and even they can only withstand so much exposure to others' troubles before it becomes too much for them. The lesson to draw is that compassion is a scarce resource. We cannot simply apply it to all of humanity without spreading ourselves too thin. We can't care about everyone the way we care about ourselves, or even about our friends and family.[18]

Some will react to this news with dismay. If it's true that we can't feel compassion for everyone who needs our help, then that suggests something awful about human nature. It means that we can't bring ourselves to do the right thing. We just don't care enough. So no matter how hard we try, we're condemned to be bad people.

This reaction is not entirely misplaced, but like the approach to morality we've been criticizing throughout this book, it overlooks something very important. Morality isn't just about helping other people as much as possible. It also requires us to fulfill our obligations to people close to us, and to ourselves. There are undoubtedly people who don't do enough to help those to whom they have no special relationship. But the mere fact that we can't focus all our attention on helping others without burning out doesn't show that we're bad, because a morally good life involves more than that. So we don't see the limits of our compassion as necessarily a bad thing. It could just be that when we're focusing too much on helping strangers, our attention is naturally drawn to the other things worth doing in life.

PATHOLOGICAL ALTRUISM

Earlier in the chapter, we mentioned a second reason some people might become busybodies: they have a pathological need to help others. How could a need to help others be pathological?

Psychoanalyst Anna Freud offered one explanation. Briefly put, she thought that, in general, altruistic behavior functions as a way for people to satisfy their desires vicariously. When people can't get what they want for themselves, Freud claimed, they turn to others and try to satisfy their desires instead.[19]

Plutarch hints at another way altruism can be pathological:

> Yet there are some who cannot bear to face their own lives, regarding these as a most unlovely spectacle, or to reflect and revolve up themselves, like a light, the power of reason, but their souls, being full of all manner of vices, shuddering and frightened at what is within, leap outwards and prowl about other people's concerns and there batten and make fat their own malice.[20]

Because they find their own lives disgusting, busybodies seek out others' problems and try to solve them. Rather than getting their own lives in order, busybodies root around in others' messes, "as a domestic fowl will often, though its own food lies near at hand, slip into a corner and there scratch where one sole barley grain perhaps appears in the dung-heap."[21] The pathology is twofold: the busybody tries to order others' lives before they've tried to order their own; and the busybody's "helping" is motivated by self-disgust, rather than, say, compassion or duty.

These explanations of busybodies only go so far, though. Take Freud's view that altruism is motivated by selfishness. This would indeed explain why the busybody's need to help could become pathological. But it isn't plausible to say that all busybodies are motivated this way, for sometimes they will try to help meet needs they themselves don't have. A busybody with a perfectly fine marriage, for example, may butt into a conversation between lovers to give them relationship advice. And setting busybodies aside, it also isn't plausible that *all* altruism is just desire-satisfaction by proxy, as Freud would have it. Similarly, Plutarch is probably right that some altruism is motivated by self-disgust, but this is unlikely to apply to all busybodies, especially those with a messiah complex who think very highly of themselves.

Modern psychologists now distinguish between healthy—or normal—altruism and pathological altruism. Healthy altruism is "the ability to experience sustained and relatively conflict-free pleasure from contributing to the welfare of others."[22] Pathological altruism, on the other hand, is "a need to sacrifice oneself for the benefit of others."[23] Another set of authors define it as "an unhealthy focus on others to the detriment of one's own needs.[24] This area of research is relatively new, and on top of that, it is difficult to classify the behavior of busybodies in general into one of these somewhat vaguely defined categories. But this emerging research program might shed some light on how altruism could be pathological.

Barbara Oakley and colleagues argue that pathological altruism emerges early in the development of one's personality. In studies of toddlers, 3 percent of children scored very high in altruistic behavior, and very low in self-actualizing behavior. The children who met *both* of these criteria "were very likely to share, care for other children, and help around the house. However, they were not at all likely to enjoy their successful helping behavior, to continue trying to complete hard tasks, or to want to do things on their own.[25] Oakley and Rachel Bachner-Melman argue that pathological altruism therefore might be linked to a deficiency in development. Drawing on Heinz Kohut's theory of development, they argue that children need to have their needs "mirrored" through others' recognition and appreciation. If this need goes unmet early in life, then people may develop an exaggerated need for responsiveness from others.[26]

The interesting part of this account, for our purposes, isn't the precise mechanism that might cause children to grow into adults who have an unhealthy need for recognition. Rather, it is that some people are disposed to be highly social, caring, and eager to receive recognition and approval from others.[27] Granting that people might be busybodies for any number of reasons, this sounds like a promising psychological profile of the kind of person we've been discussing in this chapter. This profile explains why busybodies want to help so often—they are generous, caring, and prefer to work with others. And it illuminates what busybodies hope to gain from intervening—recognition and appreciation—and why they do it so frequently—they have a deep and abiding need for that kind of positive feedback from others.

For pathological altruists, helping behavior meets a powerful psychological need that's hard to satisfy in other ways. Their attempts to help others become pathological because, in order to satisfy that need, busybodies devote excessive time and resources to helping others, overstep important social boundaries, and try to help when they're ignorant of what would do good. Again, we don't mean to suggest that busybodies all suffer from some developmental disorder. But we have tried to explain why some people are drawn to live that way, even though most everyone agrees there's something objectionable about meddling in others' affairs. We first suggested that busybodies succumb to the appealing but ultimately misguided moral conviction that we should help others as much as we can. And in this section, we've offered a minimal sketch of a psychological profile that some psychologists believe lead people to the same destination. But whatever the correct explanation, we hope you see that the path of the busybody is not one worth following.

CONCLUSION

The moralizer and the busybody err in how they ply their trade: the former in how she exercises moral criticism, the latter in how she engages in helping behavior. Each fails in their own way to mind their own business. You might wonder, though, whether people would fall so easily into the trap of moralizing or meddling if they just had better intentions. Sure, many people will be convinced by Commencement Speech Morality to seek out problems in the world and end up becoming moralizers or busybodies in the process, which we can all agree is bad. But this is often because their hearts aren't in the right place. We can do better if we just make sure we mean well. The next chapter considers this suggestion.

There is always a well-known solution to every human
problem—neat, plausible, and wrong.

H. L. Mencken, "The Divine Afflatus"

DOESN'T ANYONE CARE?

In India today, about half of the country's population of 1.3
billion people engages in open defecation. That is, instead of
using a toilet or even a simpler latrine, they defecate out in the
open—in alleys, along riverbanks, by the side of the road, in
fields near their homes, or wherever convenient.

The health consequences of this practice are severe. On a
conservative estimate, over 100,000 children under the age of
five die each year as a result of sickness from open defecation.
At the current rate, over 5 million children will die for this
reason before the practice is finally eliminated.[1] Because of
childhood sickness and the stunted growth that comes with
it, people in India are among the shortest in the world. In
2005, according to the Indian National Family Health Survey,
the average Indian man was 164 centimeters tall (about 5
feet 4 inches). For the sake of comparison, the World Health
Organization's standard for average male height in a healthy
population is 176.5 centimeters (about 5 feet 9 inches).

DOI: 10.4324/9781003459248-4

As you might expect, people who are exposed to higher rates of open defecation lag behind in education and wages, too, as they are less able to learn or work while ill. This isn't to suggest that this one practice is the cause of all misfortune in India, but life would likely be better for many people if it could be eliminated.

When you hear about a problem like the one India faces with open defecation, you might wonder, how can this be allowed to go on? Why doesn't someone do something about it? *Doesn't anyone care?*

This last question in particular is a natural thought to have. We hear about problems that seem to have straightforward solutions that people or organizations could, in principle, carry out. What stops them from doing so? Apparently, the world is suffering from an acute shortage of people who care. It is understandable that young people who want to make a difference in the world arrive at this conclusion, and armed with their good intentions, set out to address that shortage.

Aid organizations are well aware that the young people who take up the posts they offer each year think this way. Teach for America, an organization that places recent college graduates as teachers in low-income communities for two-year service terms, advertises itself like this at the top of its website: "Change the future for America's students: Seeking equity-oriented leaders who believe in helping all students reach their potential."[2] Another popular choice for public-spirited young people, the Peace Corps, provides the following description of its ideal recruit, answering the question "Is the Peace Corp Right for Me?"—"Motivated, with a passion for service. Our Volunteers are change-makers, ready to partner with communities to make a difference."[3]

It is no accident that these organizations aim their messaging specifically at the pure of heart, singling out the values and beliefs of their prospective recruits as the primary criterion of interest. The young people receiving these messages see their good intentions as the thing the world needs more of, and their primary qualification for the role of change-maker. If we can only get good people in the right place at the right time, they reason, finally the world will become a better place. Ours will be the generation that finally cares enough to make things right, they say.

But they're wrong. We don't mean that young and well-meaning people can't or won't do valuable things for the world. Of course some of them will. But caring enough doesn't have the power they think, nor is it as rare as they assume.

To be clear, our point is not to condemn people for having good intentions, or even to single out and lob criticisms at organizations that advertise their lofty goals for solving social problems. We are also not claiming that meaning well never matters. Rather, our view is that there are contexts in which it matters a great deal, and, unfortunately, we are prone to generalize from those contexts to ones where meaning well is at best unrelated to doing good. It's important for friends, family members, and romantic partners to mean well in their interactions, and to show each other that they care. But when it comes to addressing social problems, good intentions don't matter nearly as much as many people think.

The core strategy of this chapter is simple. We'll argue against two claims about the relationship between good intentions and good outcomes. First, we'll argue that meaning well is not enough to achieve good results. And second, we'll argue that meaning well isn't even required to do good. In other words, and to use the language preferred by philosophers, meaning well is neither sufficient nor necessary for promoting good outcomes.

To some, this simple approach will sound obvious, or even uninteresting. We agree that this isn't a difficult case to make. And yet, people regularly make exactly the mistakes we describe. Why do people put so much stock in good intentions when it's so easy to see that they're not that important? We'll offer a possible explanation that we think makes meaning well seem more important than it is, and thus makes the errors we point out more understandable.

MEANING WELL IS NOT ENOUGH

How can we make sense of the thought that the solution to the world's most pressing social problems lies in getting well-meaning people in place to address them? Part of the idea here seems to be that those currently in a position to bring about good outcomes just don't mean well enough, or perhaps there just aren't enough people with good intentions. Whatever the case, if we could just get the pure of heart to a place with the resources to carry out their good intentions, things would get better, and with enough of them, maybe some problems will even be solved entirely. People who mean well are the difference-maker.

Careful readers will notice that we mentioned not just good intentions, but also resources. It's technically possible that someone could hold the view that good intentions are absolutely the only thing that matters for solving problems. But outside of those mystical optimists who place extraordinary faith in the power of positive thinking to manifest good outcomes, virtually no one holds this view, and it is not worth engaging with at length. Most rational adults realize that solving problems requires resources of one kind or another—food, money, materials, social or political capital, and so on—and so we will focus our attention on the claim that if we just give good people the ability to carry out their good intentions, they will solve the world's problems.

Our view, to the contrary, is that even if well-meaning people are empowered to do what they wish to address the problems they care about, they will often fail. That is because meaning well is not enough. Simply having good intentions and taking the steps in the world that you expect will make it better does not mean you will succeed.

Technically, to show that meaning well is not sufficient for doing good, we need only come up with a single counter-example. Here's one. Suppose a babysitter, overcome with affection for the child she is caring for, decides she wants to impress her charge's parents with her attention to detail. Perhaps, she reasons, they will see how much she cares, and hire her again so she can continue to provide their child with excellent care. So, armed with her good intentions, she bathes the child in undiluted bleach, thinking that she is going above and beyond.[4] Obviously, the chemical burns that the baby would suffer are not a good outcome. Thus, good intentions (and the bleach to carry them out) are not enough.

This is just an annoying philosopher's contrived example, though. Maybe you think real people who mean well wouldn't make a mistake like that. Part of this reaction is fair. But real well-meaning people do indeed make mistakes, even if they're not usually as absurd as bathing a baby in bleach, and we have several examples for you.

First, let's return to the unusually high rate of open defecation in India. Other countries with higher rates of poverty, lower literacy rates, worse access to water, worse education systems, and poorer governance are nonetheless outperforming

India when it comes to this issue.[5] In other words, India has the resources one would expect them to need in order to eliminate open defecation, but something has stopped them from doing so. Could the problem be that people just don't care enough?

It doesn't seem so. Despite decades of interventions from both NGOs and government programs, open defecation remains a massive problem for India. Program after program has trumpeted the goal of providing access to latrines to every person in India, spending billions of dollars to realize that plan. In 1986, the Indian government announced the Central Rural Sanitation Program, aiming to promote quality of life improvements for people in rural areas, primarily by subsidizing the construction of latrines. This program was updated and renamed the Total Sanitation Campaign in 1999 and sought to provide toilet access to all inhabitants in rural areas by 2012. In 2014, the Indian government announced the Swachh Bharat Abhiyan (Clean India) mission, an extremely ambitious plan to eliminate open defecation in the country within five years. In hopes of achieving this goal, India has spent $30 billion and claims to have built over 100 million latrines. As scheduled, Prime Minister Narendra Modi declared in October of 2019—on Mohandas Gandhi's 150th birthday—that India was "open defecation free."[6]

Recent assessments of this claim show that although rates have continued to decline, the mission of an open defecation free India has not yet been accomplished. What is the problem? The same one India has faced all along, as it turns out: even when a household has access to a latrine, many still do not use it. The reasons for this behavior are complex. In their book *Where India Goes: Abandoned Toilets, Stunted Development, and the Costs of Caste*, sociologist Diane Coffey and economist Dean

Spears argue that open defecation persists in India for cultural reasons, broadly speaking.[7] Although Indians understand the germ theory of disease, many also associate defecation with a kind of religious uncleanliness.[8] Moreover, the task of emptying the latrines used in parts of the world without advanced plumbing systems is regarded in India as "Dalit work"—that is, a job suitable only for members of the lowest caste (which will be more familiar to some readers by the name "untouchables"). But even members of that caste are highly reluctant to accept work emptying the latrines, fearing ostracism and reinforcement of their low social status. And so, many people refuse to use them, instead repurposing the government-provided latrines for storage or laundry.

Unfortunately, the efforts to build so many latrines in India have not addressed these cultural issues. The good news is that access to latrines did apparently lead to increased use. People who gained access used the new latrines at roughly the same rate as those who had access before. Though as demographer Aashish Gupta and colleagues point out in their review of the program, new users of the latrines acted under coercion as the program deadline approached, and it is not clear that the change will stick.[9] Open defecation has not been eliminated in India, no matter how many times the goal has been announced, a deadline set, and victory declared.

Our point with this example is not, of course, to ridicule India for their approach to this difficult problem. Perhaps the Indian government could have achieved better results by investing in changing social attitudes about latrines, or maybe that program would have failed, too. The point to understand here is that India's good intentions and massive dedication of resources were not enough. Building 100 million latrines is a much smarter and more reasonable plan than bathing a baby in bleach, and they had ample resources to execute it. But it didn't work, because like many social problems, theirs was more complicated than just getting good people in charge and empowering them to carry out their good intentions.

But maybe you're not moved by this example. Maybe you've heard tales of Indian corruption, or you're suspicious of the Modi government, and you think this wasn't really a case of good intentions at work. Fine. Here's another example that seems clearly to be the work of the pure of heart.

The story of PlayPump starts off as heartwarming.[10] In 1989, South African advertising director Trevor Field witnessed a demonstration at an agricultural fair for a water pump that was built into a merry-go-round like the ones often found on playgrounds. He recalled seeing women in a rural village waiting for hours for the wind to pick up so that a windmill-powered pump would provide them with water to carry back to their homes, miles away. Field reasoned that this new kind of pump would solve several problems for women like those he'd seen: they could now have a water source closer to home, one that offered a technical improvement over the unreliable windmill pumps and hand pump alternatives, and, to top it off, a source of fun for the children in the village. He bought the patent for the pump, continued to develop it for several years, and in 1995 quit his job to start a charity to install the pumps in South African villages. Eventually his project attracted attention from development aid agencies, philanthropists, and celebrities, leading to tens of millions of dollars in fundraising. By 2009, PlayPump had installed over 1800 pumps in several countries across southern Africa.

Unfortunately, the story does not end so well. The pumps, it turned out, were not much fun to play with after all. If you have ever played on a merry-go-round, you might recall that there is a boring part (holding onto the handlebar and pushing the equipment to rotate until it finally gains enough momentum to move quickly on its own) and a fun part (jumping aboard while it spins). Because PlayPumps need force on the pumping mechanism to draw water, they have an unfavorable ratio of boring to fun parts in their operation. As a result, kids didn't like "playing" on them, and found alternative sources of fun. Some villages resorted to paying children to operate the pumps. There were cases of children being injured from their use and vomiting from all the spinning. In other villages, the women who used to walk to get water operated the pumps themselves, which they apparently did not enjoy. It gets even worse. The PlayPumps turned out to be less efficient than traditional hand pumps, and cost four times as much. It is safe to say, then, that meaning well didn't result in much good in this case, and quite plausibly made things worse.

Maybe you don't doubt Trevor Field's good intentions, or the badness of the outcome, but you found this example too complicated. It's just an engineering issue, you might say, or some mistake was introduced at scale. Maybe we can make one last attempt to find a simpler case.

You probably can't find a much simpler example of carrying out good intentions on a wide scale than legally requiring seatbelts in cars. In the United States prior to 1968, cars could be sold without seatbelts, and usually were. Seatbelts for adult passengers were only offered as an unpopular option on some manufacturers' vehicles starting in 1949, and the restraints only gained support from major public advocacy groups in the 1950s. We've all seen the driver's education videos of crash test dummies being thrown through windshields during simulated accidents because they weren't buckled up. All else being equal, seatbelts straightforwardly make car crashes safer. Given the historical reluctance of consumers to pay a premium for seatbelts and wear them voluntarily, it seems obvious that the mandatory inclusion of seatbelts in all cars must have had positive health and safety outcomes, and that the devices would be still more effective if laws requiring their use were enforced.

But once again, things are not so simple. Shortly after the inception of mandatory seatbelt laws, social scientists began studying their effectiveness, and the results have not been so encouraging. Economist Sam Peltzman argued in a 1975 paper that any safety improvements cars might have seen as a result of recent regulations were offset by changes in driver behavior in response to those same regulations.[11] Think of this offsetting mechanism this way. If you go climbing without a rope, you will likely be very careful and deliberate, and you would probably avoid testing the limits of what you can do successfully. But with a rope, you are free to move hastily, experiment, test your limits, and make mistakes that would have killed you had you not had safety equipment to prevent disaster. Peltzman reasoned that drivers behaved similarly after the introduction of seatbelts. With their new safety measures, drivers were more likely to speed, make dangerous lane changes, or engage in other risky behaviors. In support of his analysis, he notes that cars meeting updated safety guidelines were more likely to be involved in accidents than were cars of a similar age in the years before the change in the law. Additional studies have provided evidence of increased risk of injury and death for backseat passengers, pedestrians, and cyclists as a result of drivers' offsetting, further calling into question the efficacy of mandatory seatbelts.[12]

Some social scientists disagree with Peltzman's analysis.[13] Others have found additional support for his claims.[14] After decades of research, there is still no clear answer as to whether requiring seatbelts is, on net, an effective safety policy. There does, however, seem to be a consensus that the introduction of these laws changed peoples' behavior in unexpected and costly ways. And that is the general lesson that readers should take away from this case: apparently simple interventions can bring about unintended consequences that well-meaning people would never have seen coming, even with considerable subject-matter expertise.

In all of the real-world cases we've discussed in this section, well-meaning people have responded to a problem with a seemingly obvious solution that somehow failed to deliver the expected positive results. Why is it so difficult to solve big social problems like these? One reason is that any phenomenon that is at all complicated will be part of an intricate web of causal events. In other words, there is rarely an accurate explanation for why things happen as they do that is both very simple and reasonably complete. Instead, many factors combine in ways that we struggle to understand even after careful and painstaking study. With decades of research on the books, experts still aren't even sure what the overall effects of seatbelt laws are.

Any event, even in straightforward physical systems, will have multiple causes. But this feature is compounded in what social scientists refer to as complex systems. A complex system is one in which the behavior of one element affects many others because of the relations between those elements. In a complex system, the elements react to each other, and then react to their reactions to each other, and on and on, so that the behavior of the overall system can be highly unpredictable. One familiar example is the stock market, in which traders (and algorithms) react not only to various events, but also to the way they expect others in the market to react to those events, and how they expect others to react to their reactions, and so on.

It is difficult to intervene in a complex system and achieve one's intended result because the behavior of these systems is so hard to predict. For better or worse, society is such a system, and that is why cases of well-meaning social interventions that fail, backfire, or don't quite pan out are so easy to come by. People like to look at problems and say, "we just need to do X." But at a certain level of complexity, there is no obvious X to fill in that blank that will do the job.

Meaning well is nice, but it's not a magical guarantee of results. A well-meaning intervention might fail for any number of reasons. It might address the wrong problem, suffer from some technical failure, get derailed by others' incompetence or corruption (including the people you're trying to help), or it might just cause a weird feedback loop in our complex social system that nobody could have seen coming. The absolutely crucial thing to understand, though, is that there are no "bonus points" for throwing resources at a problem in a well-meaning way: interventions don't work just because your heart is in the right place.

MEANING WELL IS NOT REQUIRED

But maybe meaning well is crucial for doing good in a different way. Maybe, instead of being sufficient for doing good, meaning well is necessary for doing good. The claim, then, is that people who are indifferent to complex social problems will not—in fact, cannot—contribute to solving them. It's hard to bring about good consequences, especially when it comes to addressing large-scale social issues. It would be surprising if people did so by accident, the thought goes, and it seems even less likely that they'd do so without at least a thought that their actions are aiming at helping others. This is a view popular not just among laypeople. John Rawls, the most celebrated political philosopher of the 20th century once wrote that "it seems safe to assume that if a regime does not try to realize certain political values [like fair equality of opportunity], it will not in fact do so."[15]

In other words, meaning well is necessary for doing good. If we don't aim at good outcomes, we won't achieve them, just as Rawls cautions. So once again, to show that this claim is false, we need only find one counterexample. This time we need a case where someone does good without also having good intentions. Again, like our babysitter case in the previous section, we can just invent one. This time let's suppose the babysitter hates children and would harm them if she could get away with it. But she's hoping to get invited along to the family's lake house this summer so she can work on her tan. So, despising every minute of it and not actually caring about the well-being of the children, she goes through all the motions of taking care of them, and they thrive under her watch. We might not think much of this babysitter as a person. In philosophers' terms, we might downgrade our assessment of her moral character and the moral worth of her actions. Nonetheless, it must be admitted that she has done some good for the children. This in spite of the fact that her intentions were selfish: she did not care about the well-being of the children at all.

Let's also discuss a real-world example. This time we'll just give you one, but it's a big one—no more seatbelt talk. First, we'll explain the good outcome, and then we'll show how a lot of people contributed to it without meaning well. On many measures, right now is the best time to be alive in human history. Look back just 200 years, and 94 percent of the world's population was living in extreme poverty—the inflation-adjusted equivalent of less than $2 a day in purchasing power. There was nothing remarkable about the human condition 200 years ago; we had always been poor. What is remarkable is the human condition now. Today, less than 10 percent of all humans live in extreme poverty.[16] Over the same period, the literacy rate jumped from 12 percent to 86 percent.[17] Forty-three percent of people died before their fifth birthday in 1820. Now less than 4 percent do.[18] Our world has improved so drastically because in the past 200 years, we have enjoyed an unprecedented explosion in economic growth. If you're reading this book, you might not agree, but you are probably fabulously wealthy compared to almost every other human who has ever lived.

The news is not all good, of course, and we don't intend (or need) to defend every part of the story that got us here. One unfortunate feature of this sudden emergence of affluence is that some regions of the world haven't developed as quickly as others, and so have been left behind. It is popular in some circles to blame this disparity—which scholars call the Great Divergence—on colonialism or other forms of exploitation of developing countries by rich Western ones. But wealthy societies did not get rich by extracting their wealth from elsewhere. Rather, they did so by becoming more productive and thus creating more wealth.[19] We emphasize this point because for purposes of seeing what good has been done in bringing us to our contemporary condition, it is important to understand that the rich did not simply take what they have from the poor. The world economy is a positive-sum game, not a zero-sum game. The pie got bigger—much bigger.

Now, how has this process of enrichment happened, and what does it have to do with meaning well? As economist Deirdre McCloskey writes, "once upon a time we were all poor, then capitalism flourished, and now as a result we're rich."[20] Of course, capitalism is only part of the story. A lot of other pieces of a complex puzzle had to fit together just right for the Industrial Revolution to happen and spark an explosion in economic growth. But capitalism is the element that allows us to explain this example of how people can do a lot of good without meaning well. The institution of private property, the rule of law, a price system and highly specialized division of labor, and allowing people to freely trade, for example, all work together to create a positive sum game in which the size of the pie of wealth increases dramatically.

We are not claiming that capitalism is perfect.[21] But it is ingenious in this one respect: it harnesses the human tendency to pursue our own self-interest and not only renders it mostly harmless, but also directs it to promote the good of others. As Adam Smith writes famously in *The Wealth of Nations*, "It is not from the benevolence of the butcher, the brewer, or the baker that we expect our dinner, but from their regard to their own interest. We address ourselves, not to their humanity but to their self-love, and never talk to them of our own necessities but of their advantages."[22] Under the capitalist system of free exchange, we can be useful to others without caring about them at all. Many of us do it every single time we go to work, buy something from a store, pay our mortgages, or perform any other economic transaction we enter into voluntarily because it helps us achieve our ends. On the other side of these transactions is another person doing the same thing, who also need not care about us. The vast majority of our free exchanges result in both parties walking away better off than they were before. It may be impersonal and sometimes even alienating, but the result is an overall improvement in the human condition that no other form of economic organization has come close to equaling.

Capitalism has become unpopular in recent years in a way it hasn't been in the West at any other point in our lifetimes. We are aware that some of our readers will find this entire example highly off-putting. So let us make this point explicit: we are not saying that everything people do in response to the incentives a capitalist economy puts in front of them is kind, or fair, or pretty to look at. On the contrary, it is often mean, heartless, and ugly. But it is also the best way humanity has discovered of allocating resources efficiently and using them to produce good outcomes. And it works because it economizes on good intentions. Thus, it turns out, people can do a lot of good without caring about it one bit. People don't have to mean well if the system they live under appeals to their selfish nature to trick them into doing good anyway.

TWO OBJECTIONS

Even those who are not put off by our positive remarks about capitalism might find other reasons for being unimpressed with this chapter.

One objection is simply "So what?" Everyone already knows that good intentions-plus-resources don't guarantee that a plan accomplishes its aims. We also already know that people can do good in the world without being motivated by compassion or some other high-minded ideal. So, the objection goes, we have spent all this time defending two very obvious and weak claims.

If the criticism is that everyone already knows that good intentions aren't necessary or sufficient for promoting good in the world, we wouldn't be so sure. Recall, for example, John Rawls's claim that unless a society self-consciously aims at realizing its values, then it won't do so. He seems to think that at least for certain large–scale social goals, we won't achieve them unless we are properly motivated. In fact, we think many people reason this way. Perhaps they think that strictly speaking you could get lucky and accomplish great social change accidentally. But there's no good reason to count on luck. To reliably effect positive change, you must get people in charge whose hearts are in the right place.

How about our claim that good intentions aren't sufficient for good outcomes? Does everyone already know that? Again, we doubt it. The preachers of Commencement Speech Morality seem to think—and want you to think—that for all our material wealth, scientific knowledge, and technocratic expertise, what's missing is people in charge who *care*, who have the right values and goals. That extra ingredient would be enough to solve the big problems of our time.

This brings us to a second objection: isn't what's really at issue whether good intentions raise the likelihood of good outcomes? So what if good intentions don't guarantee good results? Surely it's better to have good intentions than to be apathetic, or to have bad intentions, right?

In reply, we must be clear that we aren't arguing that people shouldn't pursue projects with good intentions. Nor are we claiming that in general plans motivated with good intentions don't fare better than plans motivated by apathy or ill will. For all we've said in this chapter, we can be open to the possibility that good intentions make good outcomes more likely. Our complaint is that Commencement Speech Morality tends to produce a certain kind of activist who does think that good intentions are magic. And this confidence in the power of their good intentions leads them to moralize, meddle, and try to solve complex problems with simple solutions. If true believers in Commencement Speech Morality backpedaled and lowered their self-confidence, that would be victory enough for us.

Lest you think we are conceding too much, we conclude this section with some pessimism about even the general claim that good intentions raise the likelihood of good outcomes. Here's a reason to be skeptical that good intentions are as powerful as some think. Notice there are many kinds of good intentions one might act on. Imagine, for example, two people pursuing different kinds of solutions to a big social problem like poverty. One person might pursue a big anti-poverty policy motivated by concerns of equality, caring deeply that people feel like they live as equal citizens. Another person might pursue a very different anti-poverty policy motivated by concerns about liberty, caring deeply that people are free to live their lives as they see fit. (If you don't like one or both of these values, feel free to pick others.) We see no reason to deny that each of these people could be equally well-intentioned. But yet, and here's the problem, couldn't one or more of these equally well-intentioned ideas be a catastrophic failure? If so, what work are the good intentions themselves doing to help secure good results?

WHY DO WE CARE SO MUCH ABOUT GOOD INTENTIONS?

So far, this discussion might leave us puzzled about why people care so much about good intentions. If throwing yourself into a cause with good intentions doesn't mean you'll make a positive difference, and you can do good without even caring, then why does the appeal of meaning well have such a hold on us? Why do activists and aid organizations talk like what they really need most are idealistic, pure-hearted people to do the work that they claim will straightforwardly address social problems?

Our best guess is that there is something about human nature (for lack of a better term) that leads us to place a lot of emphasis on whether someone is well-meaning. If you think about small-scale social interactions, it makes perfect sense to feel this way. Who wants to hang out with someone who's kind of a jerk? Who would be eager to trust someone who seems cold and uncaring? How many times has a friend assured you that someone they're going to introduce you to is "a nice guy"? It would probably be easier to remember the number of times they didn't.

In support of this conjecture, note that early humans lived in small groups that depended on their ability to cooperate with the same people repeatedly. In these conditions, it was vital to an individual's survival that he be able to trust other group members, and that he could show them that they could trust him. Reliance on, and anxiety about, trust has thus been an essential part of human social life for a very long time. It would not be surprising, then, if this feature of our species' culture influenced our evolution and left modern humans with a tendency to judge peoples' suggestions for solving problems based on whether they seem trustworthy. And the fact that a person seems to be well-meaning is evidence that they are trustworthy, and thus can help you.

The trouble with continuing to rely on these judgments is that we no longer live in relatively simple small group settings where any competent adult can observe what is happening and figure out whether it is good or bad and what to do about it. In short, it seems that we are naturally inclined to project the dynamics of small-scale interactions onto massively complex social systems that cannot be interacted with in the same way. Our distant ancestors knew more or less what would happen if they made a minor change to the management of their small village economy. Now even experts with decades of experience are unsure what the outcome of most policy interventions will be—or at least they should be unsure. Meanwhile, we are still relying on our judgments of affective trust—our sense of whether a person can be counted on to care or be emotionally supportive—when we should be distinguishing those judgments from those of cognitive trust—whether a person is technically competent in the relevant field, if there are any such people.

Whether this evolutionary story for how we got to be this way is apt or not, people are susceptible to what psychologists call attribution errors.[23] That is, we tend to overemphasize the role of individuals' psychological traits—their moral character or personality—in explaining their behavior and pay insufficient attention to the constraints of the situation in which they are acting. This would explain why people look at a problem that leaders and organizations are currently failing to solve and are tempted by the thought that there's something wrong with those leaders and organizations, rather than pausing to consider that the situation might be more complicated than they realize.

CONCLUSION

Many people are likely drawn to work for activist groups, non-profit companies, and other organizations promising to make change because they offer an outlet for their good intentions, which will surely be effectively wielded against the social problems they care about. What we've tried to show here is that meaning well is not as powerful a force as many might hope.

The past three chapters have been negative. We saw the downsides of minding others' business by being a moralizer or busybody. And we've argued here that good intentions don't magically ensure good outcomes when we attempt to solve big social problems. Engaging in the problems and affairs of others often has significant costs. We should be wary of minding others' business.

But this is only half the story. Minding your own business means not minding the business of others. But it also means minding *your own* business. What is your business? And why is it OK to devote your energies to those things? In the next three chapters, we explain why minding your own business, far from being selfish, can contribute to a generous, noble, and peaceful life.

5

> Whoever is uprooted himself uproots others. Whoever is
> rooted himself, doesn't uproot others.
>
> Simone Weil, *The Need for Roots*

"YOU GOT TO GET OUT THERE"

In her 2015 commencement speech to the University of Wisconsin, journalist Katie Couric told graduates, "You got to get out there and get yourself noticed." Get out where, one wonders. And noticed by whom?

Some students go for it. They start tech companies and build a huge Twitter following. Others become social media influencers. Some move overseas to build wells for the poor and get profiled by *The New Yorker*.

But others ignore Katie Couric, or at least they ignore this kind of advice. They finish school, get married, start a family, and settle down somewhere. They don't try to get "out there" and make a name for themselves. They're satisfied to live in relative obscurity. They go to work, pay their taxes, raise their children, coach softball, join the Kiwanis club, practice their religion, and take care of their aging parents. Often, they don't stray far from their families. The median distance between Americans and their mothers is only 18 miles. 80 percent live within a two-hour drive.[1]

DOI: 10.4324/9781003459248-5

Far from stepping into the public eye and fixing society's big problems, many ordinary people put down roots and become attached to their neighborhoods and towns. They devote their social energies to life at home. They spend time alone: fishing, reading, walking. Each of these—putting down roots, devotion to home life, and solitude—is a way to mind your own business. We'll discuss home and solitude in the coming chapters. Here, we will explain why it's OK to put down roots.

THE NEED FOR ROOTS

In 1943, French philosopher and activist Simone Weil died. Unwell in mind and body, Weil starved herself to death at a sanatorium in Kent, England. She was 34.

Weil was, and remains, a polarizing figure. Charles de Gaulle once called her "insane."[2] Albert Camus thought she was "the only great spirit of our times."[3] The poet T.S. Eliot couldn't "conceive of anybody's agreeing with all of her views, or of not disagreeing violently with some of them."[4] Weil's views are often radical, even paradoxical.[5]

Weil had been living in London in the years leading up to her death. Hitler invaded France three years prior, and Weil aided the French resistance from across the English Channel. Free France, the French government-in-exile led by Charles de Gaulle, operated from England trying to subvert the Nazis and the Nazi-friendly French government. Although victory in Europe was still years away, Free France was already concerned about the future of their country were the Nazis defeated. How could they rebuild social and political life after the war? Could France resist fascism in the future? Free France asked Weil to address these questions, to which she devoted the final months of her short life.

After her death, Albert Camus compiled Weil's notes into a book and published them. L'Enracinement appeared in 1949. The first English translation, titled The Need for Roots, appeared in 1952. It is a perplexing, sometimes frustrating book. In it, Weil describes the "needs of the soul." Although more difficult to identify than the needs of the body—housing, clothing, food, and water—the needs of the soul are no less important. Weil's list of the soul's needs includes order, liberty, obedience, responsibility, equality, hierarchism, honor, punishment, freedom of opinion, security, risk, private and collective property, and truth. In her view, a good society meets these needs and thereby nourishes souls. Bad societies fail to nourish them. At worst, a society destroys souls. That's what the fascists did to France. Weil argues that to rebuild their nation and to guard against another invasion, the French must build a society that meets not just the needs of the body, but the needs of the soul.

Much of the book is devoted to one need of the soul in particular, what she calls rootedness. "To be rooted," she writes, "is perhaps the most important and least recognized need of the human soul. It is one of the hardest to define."[6] Perhaps realizing this difficulty, Weil did not say much about what it means to be rooted. Her remarks on rootedness are brief and impressionistic. (We will return to some of these remarks later.)

But we can say more about what it means to put down roots. We suspect most readers have a general sense of what people mean when they say they want to put down roots, or when they express concern that a recent move left them feeling uprooted. Rootedness is one of those ideas that seems simple enough, but when you try to pin it down, you realize, as Weil did, that it's difficult to define.

Let's keep things simple. Think about the metaphor of rootedness. A plant's roots attach it to some place, securing it at a location. Roots help nourish the plant, delivering water and minerals from the soil. But the roots also "give back," preserving the integrity of the soil and preventing erosion. It's easy to make too much of metaphors, this one included. But these simple observations suggest a starting point for understanding how people can also be rooted:

> A rooted person is someone attached to a place, who receives benefits from it, and who responsibly preserves the good things there.

Let's say a bit more about these three aspects of rootedness before we argue that being rooted is one way to mind your own business.

PLACE ATTACHMENT

The unrooted lack a meaningful bond to a place. Some unrooted people are intentional nomads, moving from one city and job to another, constantly looking for new opportunities, better relationships, and more exciting experiences. The nomad doesn't commit to a place and has no plans to do so. Many live their lives this way, always with an eye on the next adventure.

Unlike nomads, some people's rootlessness is put upon them. They have been uprooted. Think of the child whose family moves constantly. Or the precariously employed who move from place to place just to find work. Refugees are uprooted from their homes.

Unlike the unrooted, who merely reside somewhere, the rooted have formed an attachment to the place they live. This attachment to a place is the first aspect of rootedness. Place attachment is not, we should be clear, an all or nothing matter. It's a spectrum. You've probably had the experience of, upon moving to a new place, feeling totally disconnected from it. It might have even felt distant, cold, and alienating. But with any luck, you came to know the place and feel at home there. You can also simultaneously have different levels of attachment to multiple places. The retired couple feels more attached to the hometown where they raised a family than the beach town they visit every summer. And they're more attached to the beach town than to Madrid, where they honeymooned.

Over the last 50 years, psychologists have tried to make sense of our bonds to places.[7] We can distill much of this research by thinking about place attachment according to a very simple model: place attachment occurs when a person or group of people has a particular sort of relationship to a place.[8] Let's explore each of these three aspects: the person, the place, and the relationship between them.

Place attachment can happen between a single person and a place. You might have a meaningful connection to the city you live in, or the vacation spot you visited every summer growing up. But groups can also be attached to a place. A local culture or religious community experiences a bond to an area that has developed cultural or religious significance throughout its history. There is often a shared sense of "we" among people who feel attached to such a place.

Sometimes a person feels attached to a place merely as a physical location. A hidden spot on a particular lake or a hiking path in a local forest can take on a special meaning. But often people are attached not merely to a geographical place or landscape, but to the combination of that place and the people there. Think of some place you're attached to: a coffee shop, a hometown, a neighborhood. Your connection is not merely to the physical space but also to the people you know and interact with there. Neither is this attachment merely to the people, though. Rather, it is to the *place that has these people*. Many of us have had the experience of returning to a place that once held meaning for us only to feel disappointed upon realizing its familiar cast has been replaced. Similarly, it can be jarring to encounter a familiar group of people in a radically different setting. So, when we speak of a place, we mean the combination of a location with certain of its social aspects.

To become attached to a place, you need some direct experience of it.[9] Neither of your authors is attached to Anchorage, Alaska. We've never been there. Places you've never been or places that are just too big to experience (say, the Pacific Ocean) are not good candidates for the type of place we have in mind. When we talk about putting down roots and feeling attached to a place, we mean a smaller physical space. But not too small. Rooted people aren't merely attached to their house. Rather, the kind of place we have in mind is roughly the size of your town. Or if you live in a big city, your part of town.[10]

Place attachment is a bond. This bond has both an attitudinal dimension and a behavioral dimension. Let's start with the attitudes. Place attached people have a characteristic set of positive emotions, beliefs, memories, and desires about a place. For example, someone attached to their town might feel pride when talking to visitors about it, anticipation and comfort when returning home from a trip, and grief when moving away for a new job. A sense of familiarity is also crucial to place attachment. Chances are you'll be more attached to the place you've lived for years than the Tallahassee Holiday Inn Express where you once spent an evening. People strongly attached to a place have fond memories of it and want to see it preserved. These attitudes can be so important to a person that they become incorporated into how someone thinks about himself. A place can become part of who you are.

Place attachment also has a behavioral dimension. Place attached people tend to move less often than the unattached. This doesn't mean they never leave—for a vacation, perhaps. But when they do leave, they'll eventually want to return. We are college professors and for the first few weeks of every new academic year, college freshmen get homesick.[11] They want, not just to see their families, but to return to a place that holds special meaning to them.

One of the enduring themes of literature is the return to a meaningful place, especially home. In Homer's epic poem, the *Odyssey*, we learn that Odysseus the King of Ithaca has spent ten years fighting the Trojan War. Eager to return home, he is delayed another ten years because he's angered Poseidon, god of the sea. His voyage home is the plot of the *Odyssey*.

> Nevertheless I long—I pine, all my days—
> to travel home and see the dawn of my return.
> And if a god will wreck me again on the wine-dark sea,
> I can bear that too, with a spirit tempered to endure.
> Much have I suffered, labored long and hard by now
> in the waves and wars. Add this to the total—
> bring the trial on![12]

And the trials were plenty: Poseidon wrecking his ship, Circe the witch's poisonings and seductions, more ship-wrecking, cannibals, the singing Sirens, and the monsters Scylla and Charybdis. Odysseus declines the offer of immortality from the nymph Calypso, who detains him on the island Ogygia for seven years as she tries to make him her husband. Eventually, he finds himself washed up on Ithaca's shore. Disguised, Odysseus kills the suitors trying to marry his wife, Penelope, who has long presumed him dead. When he finally reveals himself to her, they retire to the bed he had built for their wedding decades before. The bed, which Odysseus had carved from the stump of an olive tree, was still rooted into the ground.

We can think of place attachment, then, as a bond between people and the place where they live, characterized by a sense of pride, familiarity, comfort, and a desire to remain. Attachment is just one aspect of being rooted in a place, though. Rooted people are not only bonded to a place, they also enjoy its benefits.

THE BENEFITS OF ROOTEDNESS

On April 3, 1974, an F5 category tornado leveled the small Ohio city of Xenia, population 25,000. Barreling through the center of town, the tornado killed 32 and injured 1,300. It leveled hundreds of homes, and many parts of the city had to be rebuilt from the ground up. City planners proposed new zoning maps that would fix problems that had previously plagued the city. But the residents rejected them, and the newly rebuilt Xenia looked just like the old Xenia.[13]

St. Mark's Campanile is a bell tower in Venice, Italy. At over 300 feet, it is the tallest building in the city and a famous landmark. It's beautiful: a red brick tower, limestone belfry, copper spire, and a gilded weathervane of the archangel Michael. Construction began in the 10th century and was eventually completed in 1514. Four hundred years later, in 1902, St. Mark's Campanile collapsed into a pile of rubble. Days later the local council voted unanimously to rebuild the tower exactly as it was, with some structural improvements (as you might imagine, engineering had improved in the intervening thousand years).

The people of Xenia and Venice shared a desire for continuity. In response to a radical change to a place they loved, they remade things as they once were. Continuity of place helps make life predictable and coherent. The unrooted must continue to learn new places: where to buy food, what areas are unsafe, when traffic is bad, and so on. Rooted people have mastered these place-facts and don't have to give them much thought. Even with the Internet, it still can take time to learn what others know because they put down roots.

Continuity of place provides a stable "background" against which people can situate the fragmented or unpredictable aspects of life. In a span of just ten years, you might experience a new child (or three), a new job, the death of a friend, and rapidly shifting political winds. You change too, as you lose or gain religion, deal with the effects of aging, and navigate health challenges. Place attachment, however, helps us "integrate various life experiences into a coherent life story," writes psychologist Maria Lewicka.[14] In the face of life's constant changes, that coherent story enables "a smooth transition from one identity stage to another in the life course."[15] It may not surprise you that place attached people report a higher sense of coherence than the unattached—their lives make more sense to them.[16]

The unrooted must continue to meet new people and learn whom to trust. But the rooted enjoy a more predictable social life. They learn, the hard way or by reputation, who can be trusted to do car repairs. Your neighbor might be tempted to take advantage of you if you aren't going to be around for long. But when people are committed to living in the same place for a long time, their incentives change. Repeated inter-actions make reciprocity more rational. This likely explains why, compared to the unattached, place-attached people tend to be more trusting of others.[17]

One day in 2020, I (Brandon) was lecturing online. I could see that my left eyelid was starting to swell. My throat tightened and I couldn't talk. I was having a severe allergic reaction. I didn't have Benadryl and didn't want to drive to the emergency room. So, I walked across the street to my neighbors. They medicated me so I didn't asphyxiate because I'd gotten dust in my eye.

These kinds of interactions are common for rooted people. Place attachment provides a ready-made support structure when things go wrong. Local friends can be trusted to watch your kids if you need to spend a few days in the hospital. Neighbors can let your dogs out if you're working late, or get your mail when you're out of town. These resources are called social capital, and rooted people have more of it.

In 1961, psychologist Harry Harlow published a study that no modern university would allow. He separated infant rhesus monkeys from their mothers. He then provided each infant monkey with one of two artificial "mothers": one mother made of wire and wood and the other made of soft foam and cloth. The infant monkeys spent much more time with the cloth mother than the wire mother, and clung to the cloth mother when afraid, even when only the wire mother had milk.[18] Harlow's experiments have shaped decades of work on interpersonal attachment, especially between mothers and their children. We form attachments not primarily to meet physiological needs, but to satisfy our needs for comfort and security.

Similarly, the places where we put down roots can be a source of comfort and security.[19] One reason that rootedness provides comfort and security is that, as we have already discussed, being attached to a place provides a sense of continuity. For the rooted, navigating the world is less taxing and it's perceived as less threatening. Rooted people also don't have to worry about moving, a common source of much distress. Picking up and uprooting yourself, your family, your belongings, your friendships, and your affections for a place not yet known or loved is one of life's most anxiety-producing events. (You might even feel a twinge of anxiety reading this as you imagine doing it yourself.) Moving may be especially harmful to children. A large Danish study of over 1.4 million people suggests that frequent moving as a child is associated with increased risk of violent offending, attempted suicide, and substance misuse.[20] Putting down roots can be not only a source of comfort and security for oneself, but an important form of care for one's children.

Rooted people are not only attached to a place, but they also receive the benefits it offers: continuity and predictability, increased social trust and social capital, and comfort and security. This list certainly isn't complete, and people will differ with respect to their needs. Some people tend to do just fine living as rootless nomads (or at least this is how they prefer to live their lives). We have no truck with them. Our aim is not to convince everyone to put down roots, but to argue that it's OK for you to put down roots. Before we do that, though, we need to talk about the last aspect of rootedness.

THE RESPONSIBILITIES OF ROOTEDNESS

In many parts of the world, soil erosion creates massive problems. Wind and rain remove nutrient-rich topsoil and deposit it in rivers, lakes, and oceans. Much erosion occurs naturally. It's how we got the Grand Canyon. But by constantly uprooting the trees and plants that protect soil from the elements, industrial agriculture and deforestation have made matters worse. The result is deteriorated farmland and polluted water, as dirt and pesticides make their way into rivers and lakes.

As early as 1928, the U.S. Department of Agriculture called soil erosion a "national menace."[21] The U.S. is estimated to be losing soil ten times faster than the natural replenishment rate.[22] But the problem is global. China and India are losing soil at 30–40 times the rate of natural replenishment. Worldwide, erosion has been estimated to cause $400 billion in damage.

Soil erosion on farmland can be easily reduced by planting "cover crops" in the off-season, when fields would otherwise sit empty. Not only do these various grasses or clovers shield the soil from wind, but their roots protect the soil from rainwash. The diameter, strength, length, surface area, and especially the microscopic "hairs" that many roots possess, bind soil together and reduce erosion.[23]

Unfortunately, erosion of a more general sort affects other areas of life. Without protection and care, the valuable things around us—including those things that give life meaning—fall into disorder and degradation.

Take, for instance, your local habitat. If you put down roots in a small town or in the countryside, your habitat will be the natural landscape: fields, forests, and bodies of water. If you put down roots in a suburb or large city, much of your habitat will be things humans have created: buildings, lawns, sidewalks, gardens, and parks. Many things in your habitat are good and worth keeping. This doesn't mean they are perfect. But they provide beauty, order, and function. Without them life would be much worse.

Habitats do not preserve themselves, though. They are not time capsules.[24] Simply leaving things alone won't maintain beauty, order, or function. To ignore them is to guarantee erosion. Some erosion occurs naturally, as weeds and invasive plant species overtake public gardens. Building façades crumble. Sometimes we speed up the erosion ourselves, as when developers replace beautiful architecture with the cheap, ugly, and crudely utilitarian.

Erosion also threatens our institutions, those forms of social organization that possess their own rules and functions. Examples of institutions include libraries, elementary schools, the legal system, houses of worship, hospitals, mutual aid societies, businesses, the postal service, journalistic outlets, gyms, running clubs, police departments, markets, professional sports leagues, and universities. For most of us, the first institution we experience is the family.

Institutions, like our habitats, are ubiquitous. As the "building blocks of the social order," they form the backdrop of our lives.[25] We go through life relying on them, assuming they will be there when needed. For most of our readers, you'll wake up tomorrow and assume you can send your kids to functioning schools, that you won't find strangers living in your garage, and that the cashier at the local grocer will trade you beer for cash.

The importance of institutions cannot be overstated. This is because institutions are, as economist Douglass North explains, "humanly devised constraints that structure political, economic, and social interaction."[26] Consider a local marketplace. It will have hours of operation, a physical space that encourages some forms of activity and prohibits others, and shops or merchants whose special skills influence the local clientele and culture. By constraining our behavior, institutions create the possibility of a peaceful and predictable social order. They help us coordinate with others to solve problems and provide environments in which humans can find meaning and meet basic needs. Try imagining what your life would be like without them.

Unfortunately, many people don't have to imagine. Globally, tens of millions of people live in failed states, where the economy has collapsed, the government has stopped providing basic services, crime runs rampant, and people generally don't trust each other. Commentators often cite Syria, Yemen, and Somalia as failed states. Racked by civil war, these places cannot serve as suitable sites for putting down roots. It is no coincidence these states produce so many refugees.

Failed states serve as a vivid and useful reminder that peaceful and well-functioning social orders are fragile. Of course, at some level everyone knows this. But what may be less obvious is that you need not live in a failed state to be at risk of erosion affecting your own local institutions. Without preservation and upkeep, local institutions are as liable to erosion as local habitats. Although the Fraternal Order of Eagles—the organization responsible for the creation of Mothers' Day in the United States—undoubtedly continues to do good work at their 1500 local "aeries," their membership numbers have been stagnant for the past 40 years. The Eagles are certainly not as prominent they used to be when U.S. Presidents were counted among their members. Unless something changes, their days of exerting major influence over our culture will lie in the past. Still, they are a relative success story. Many such organizations do disappear altogether.[27] Sometimes an institution continues to exist but people lose trust in it. It stops serving its function or its leaders are corrupt. Examples of such institutions are bound to spark strong feelings in some readers, but some plausible cases include the Catholic Church after its pedophilia scandal, the Boy Scouts of America after its own such scandal, and the American Civil Liberties Union after its transformation from an organization devoted to defending the constitutional rights of even the most unpopular Americans to one more focused on current progressive causes, even when they conflict with rights the organization previously would have defended.

The key point is that our habitats and institutions do not preserve themselves. People must do it. This might seem like a trivial observation. Maybe so. But focusing on it will help us see why putting down roots gives us responsibilities, and further, why this is the sort of business to which it's OK to devote oneself.

In the 5th century A.D., Western Europe experienced world historic levels of social erosion. In the span of 100 years, a massive empire was laid to ruin. The Visigoths entered the Western Roman Empire in 376 from Scandinavia. In 410, Alaric, the Visigoth king, sacked Rome, destroying public buildings and burning or stealing all manner of art and books. The Huns, Gauls, and Vandals took their turns attacking Rome, too. By 476, the barbarian military leader Odoacer deposed the last Roman Emperor Romulus Augustus—a child—and made himself King of Italy. Throughout Western Europe, the treasures of classical literature were at risk of being lost as an empire imploded.

Though we can't be sure how great the threat was, the successor kingdoms to the Western Roman Empire apparently had little interest in the poetry of Homer and Virgil, the history of Herodotus, the speeches of Cicero, and the philosophy of Plato and Aristotle. And yet these works were saved. Some were preserved by the Byzantine Empire in the East. And in Ireland in the West, mostly outside the reach of barbarians, a small band of Irish monks trained by Saint Patrick and Saint Columba preserved the literary treasures of classical Europe. These monks sat in their frigid beehive huts along the rocky Irish coast and copied the literature delivered to them from the continent. The Irish may not have saved civilization.[28] But they certainly saw something valuable that needed preserving and got to work.

We've now come to the third aspect of rootedness: preserving the good stuff around you. Being rooted is not simply a matter of being attached to a place and receiving its benefits. Rootedness also means giving something back to the place that sustains you. Again, the metaphor of rootedness is illuminating. A plant's roots prevent soil erosion. Your putting down roots prevents social erosion. Rootedness therefore involves taking responsibility to give back to one's place.

Consider historic districts with preservation laws. People who live in such districts are required to maintain their properties according to the guidelines for historical accuracy. They must submit their plans to replace doors or windows to a commission for review and approval, for instance. Additions and repairs to homes must be of the appropriate style and use approved materials. Failure to comply with these requirements is punishable by fines, and courts are empowered to compel owners to follow the rules of their district.[29] Naturally, it would be cheaper and easier for residents to maintain their homes however they wish, using modern materials. But if they did so, the character of their neighborhood would change. And at least according to those who have chosen to live in these areas because of their historic feel, an important aspect of their place would be destroyed.

Not all erosion can be prevented, of course. Even the best things will eventually be bulldozed, shut down, or swallowed by an earthquake. Some local habitats and institutions are not worth preserving. And sometimes there are perfectly good reasons to destroy things. Schools where mass shootings occur are often razed and rebuilt, for example.[30] But rooted people feel a shared responsibility to preserve the good things around them. They want to prevent erosion, or at least delay it.

It's easy to think of rootedness as something that happens at a time—that to be rooted is to be attached to a place now, to have our needs met and to give back to our place now. But Simone Weil didn't think this was exactly right.

> A human being has roots by virtue of his real, active and natural participation in the life of a community which preserves in living shape certain particular treasures of the past and certain particular expectations of the future.[31]

Rootedness extends through time. Weil imagines a lineage of people connected to one another because they share and will continue to share a place. In Weil's terms, the rooted preserve the "treasures of the past" and "expectations of the future." In our terms, being rooted means preserving your local habitats and institutions in the face of erosion. Our ancestors dedicated large parts of their often short lives to building the habitats and institutions that shape our lives. And like the Irish monks who copied ancient poetry onto folds of sheepskin, any rooted person who has inherited a good habitat or institution can help preserve them so they can be given to others still. It is our rootedness, Weil writes, that "constitutes the sole agency for preserving the spiritual treasures accumulated by the dead, the sole transmitting agency by means of which the dead can speak to the living."[32]

ROOTEDNESS AS MINDING YOUR BUSINESS

As we saw in the first half of this book, there is no single way to mind others' business. One can be a moralizer, for instance, or a busybody. Similarly, there is no single way to mind your own business. For not only is there no one thing that is your business, there is no one way to mind it.

One way to mind your own business, however, is to be rooted: to be attached to a place, benefit from it, and responsibly preserve its habitat and institutions. When you put down roots, your local habitat and institutions become part of your business. You might have expected a defense of minding your own business to amount to an argument for keeping to yourself or living as you please. In short, you may have come looking for something more radical. But this book is not called *Why It's OK to be a Rugged Individualist* or *Why It's OK to be Selfish*. We defend an ordinary kind of life against those who tell people—especially young people—that their lives are second-rate if they aren't out there changing the world and making a name for themselves. Instead, many people put down roots.

Are they wrong to do so? No. It's OK to put down roots, at least for the vast majority of us. Being rooted is crucially important to our welfare. Rootedness offers a sense of security, comfort, and familiarity. It reduces anxiety and fear, promotes social trust, and sustains close friendships. The sense of stability that comes from having a "home base" is what gives many people the freedom and confidence to explore and travel.[33] If we have any duties to ourselves at all, putting down roots is a good candidate, for it's by becoming rooted that so much of what is good in life is made available to us.

If this was all rootedness amounted to, it would be morally acceptable. But as we have seen, rootedness also involves taking some responsibility for preserving the good things around you. That rootedness involves this form of reciprocity makes it even clearer that putting down roots is, far from being blameworthy, an admirable way to live.

Of course, one can be a moralizer or a busybody in one's local community, too. Being devoted to the health of our habitats and institutions doesn't inoculate us from the temptations of minding other's business. Even so, rootedness can be a kind of antidote to Commencement Speech Morality. Many people—perhaps especially young people—are enamored by the thought that if someone isn't out there making a name for themselves and changing the world then they are not doing much good—or worse, that they are selfish. Rootedness disabuses us of this lie. For many of us, we can do considerable good in the world, given our limited time, energy, knowledge, and expertise, by putting down roots and sustaining the good things that others have handed to us.

If you put down roots, you probably won't become famous. No more than a handful of people might even know what you're doing. As sociologist Edward Shils observed, "founders are praised; innovators are praised, but not those who have maintained what the innovators created."[34] Commencement Speech Morality encourages young people to be Founders and Innovators. (It is perhaps not surprising that commencement speakers are often themselves Founders and Innovators.) There is nothing wrong with being a Founder or Innovator. But not everyone can be one. Nor would we want that. Society needs Maintainers. You just won't be famous for it. If you want to be famous for changing the world, maintenance is a bad bet. But if you have other goals—to live a worthwhile life or leave good things for others after you are gone—then preserving the good things around you is a sound investment.

It's of course possible that your attempts to do good locally will fail or backfire. There are no guarantees. But aiming to maintain your local institutions and habitat enjoys two advantages over grander world-improvement schemes. First, as we saw in Chapter 4, the world is unimaginably complex. Such extremely high levels of complexity make it difficult to know how to solve large-scale problems, especially those problems that beset people from different cultures, religions, and languages. Your local world is complex too, but much less so. You're more likely to hit upon a beneficial solution to a problem and do good at lower levels of social complexity. Chances are, you'll do better at maintaining your local library or improving municipal snow removal than devoting your time to national political causes, let alone international ones.

A second benefit of directing your energies locally is that you'll be more careful because you have skin in the game. It's easier to buy into risky world-changing schemes when you have little to lose. You don't have to pay the cost if disaster ensues. One continually fascinating feature of contemporary political life is that many people advocate for policies they would never dream of subjecting themselves to. But not so for the rooted: not only do you get up close and personal knowledge of how things are playing out, but you have to consider seriously whether you want to live in a world of your own making. Instead of conscripting others into your social experiments, you must volunteer to be the test subject.

CONCLUSION

It's OK to put down roots. Usually, it doesn't even matter where you do it. Letting your community fall into disorder and disrepair doesn't help anyone around you. Rooted people help prevent this social erosion, and they do so by minding their own business.

Home is where one starts from.

T.S. Eliot, "East Coker," *Four Quartets*

HOME LIFE

The home is not simply a physical structure, though it is not less than that. The home also includes the people who live there, and the personal "belongings" those people keep there. The ancient Greeks had a name for this holistic idea of the home: the *oikos*.

For most readers, your apartment, dormitory, or house will be your home. You may live with others or alone. Your home is one of the few places—maybe the only place—on the face of the earth where you enjoy immense freedom. You may create a space that suits you and where you feel comfortable. Within very wide limits, others may not tell you how to arrange your home. You decide what to do there, and when to do it. That's your business, and not anyone else's (except for those you share a home with, who, after a certain age, might also have a say).

One way to mind your business is by attending to your home. Of course, not all ways of doing so are morally good, let alone admirable. But it is certainly admirable to create a

DOI: 10.4324/9781003459248-6

safe, peaceful, and welcoming home. We can call such a place a *good home*. A good home provides its inhabitants with relative safety. Those who live there can reasonably expect not to be physically harmed, either by intruders or by anyone else who lives there. Good homes are also peaceful insofar as they are generally low stress and not chaotic. The inevitable conflicts of home life are dealt with in productive and healthy ways. Good homes are welcoming. Private, but not fully closed off from the world, good homes are places for friendship and hospitality.[1] Many people mind their own business precisely by focusing their efforts on making a home for themselves and their families. We can call a *home life* one that involves devoting significant time and resources to creating and maintaining a good home.

A good home takes effort to create and maintain. At one level, everyone knows this. Homes are physical places that require maintenance and upkeep. People devote considerable time and resources to making repairs, cleaning, decorating, and adding onto their homes. Americans spend more than $400 billion a year on home renovations and repairs.[2] Each year, American college students dish out $6 billion to furnish their dorms.[3] Everyone recognizes that good homes require time and resources: furniture to buy, walls to decorate, roofs to replace, mice to kill, and sinks to clean.[4]

Good homes require more than physical attention, however, because the *oikos* is more than just a physical object. Good homes also demand personal and social attention: kindness, care, generosity, healthy communication, and love. A kitchen renovation doesn't make a home safe, peaceful, or welcoming. Good homes are not made accidentally or automatically, either. Often, they aren't made at all, as many can unfortunately attest. Creating a good home takes considerable time and attention. It is easy to underestimate the time and attention that must be diverted from other perfectly worthwhile projects to make a good home.

Commencement Speech Morality conflicts with these thoughts about the importance of home. The world is full of evils, its proponents intone. Some exist in your town. Yet there are only so many hours in the day. How can you justify devoting significant amounts of time and resources to home life when there are so many serious problems in the world? Isn't it near-sighted and selfish?

Ordinary Morality, on the other hand, licenses and even encourages devoting time and resources to home life. Most people aren't concerned about the morality of spending time relaxing at home after work. They spend hours playing with their kids on the living room floor. On weekends, they have friends, neighbors, or relatives over for dinner. They decorate their homes with furniture and art that make them feel at home. Of course, not everyone devotes this much attention to their home. Just as we saw in the previous chapter that not everyone has a particularly strong desire to put down roots, not everyone makes home life a high priority. But of course many do, and for the vast majority of people, the thought never occurs to them that it might be morally wrong to spend much of their time and resources on the home. In fact, it might seem that we are attacking a strawman: surely no one would criticize this way of life.

It's true that commencement speeches themselves are unlikely to decry home life explicitly. But for young people who are told to get out there, do big things, make a name for themselves, and change the world, home life can seem small, insignificant, even a comparative waste of one's limited time on earth. We doubt that few students who hear these admonitions feel energized to get to work making a good home. And for those who ultimately choose home life, they may still feel they've chosen a second-rate, if not morally suspect, life path. Home life looks like small potatoes compared to effecting political change on the big stage.

But home life, far from being second-rate, is morally admirable. Although this is a widely held view, it is not a widely defended one, especially among philosophers. You will rarely find contemporary philosophers writing on the importance of the home or family, let alone standing up for them. Our goal in this chapter is to speak in favor of home life. There are good reasons to devote considerable time and resources to creating and maintaining a good home. Young people especially should not feel pressured by professors or politicians or parents to forsake dreams of home life in service to national politics, or upsetting the status quo, or starting a revolution.

Our discussion of creating a good home or "home life" might lead some readers to think that we are talking about stay-at-home parents or homemakers—those who do not work outside the home and instead devote much of their lives to cleaning, cooking, child-rearing, and shopping for the family. But there is nothing about home life as such that requires being a homemaker. College students, working singles and parents, and empty nesters can all, in their own way, create good homes. Furthermore, people from across the political spectrum can agree on the importance of good homes.

REFUGE

There is an old Chinese tradition of the literati garden. Over the centuries, these gardens varied in size and function, but the basic idea was to create a natural landscape on the property near your home. Literati gardens were places to walk, contemplate, read, or study. One could even invite friends over to enjoy the retreat from the social world.

The traditional literati garden illustrates how a good home—one that is safe, peaceful, and welcoming—can be a refuge. A home is a refuge because it provides a retreat from the public world. At home we can escape the bad, dangerous, stressful, and unhealthy: would be attackers, inclement weather, and workplace drama. Homes also provide refuge from things that are fine in themselves, but from which it is good to take a break: norms of professionalism, rules of public etiquette, and expectations of workplace productivity. However, homes do not merely offer an escape from public life. Homes also provide a refuge for the cultivation of important private goods. In the home you can find a positive environment of support, encouragement, freedom, and rest.

Let's be more specific about how the home provides refuge. Most obviously, home is a physical refuge. It offers protection from physical threats and provides physical benefits. Some physical threats are natural—inhospitable weather and dangerous wildlife chief among them. Other physical threats are personal. Homes mitigate the risk of bodily harm, theft, and violations of privacy. Among their physical benefits, homes function as a reliable place for sustenance and rest. Put simply, it's where you keep your food and where you sleep. These might seem like trite observations. But they would not be taken for granted by our ancestors throughout virtually all of human history. And they are not now taken for granted by billions of people for whom reliable protection from natural and personal threats is a daily concern.

Homes also provide psychological refuge from the stress-causing spheres of public life, particularly the workplace and politics. Forty percent of U.S. workers say that their job is "very or extremely stressful." A quarter report that their job is "the number one stressor in their lives."[5] Fifty-seven percent of Americans say that politics is a very or somewhat significant source of stress in their lives.[6] Politics has an unfortunate tendency to infiltrate private life, with 20 percent reporting that politics has damaged a friendship, and 17 percent saying that politics has damaged family relations or made their home life less pleasant.[7] But if you manage it well, home can provide a refuge from the stresses of work and politics.[8]

The ability for home to be a refuge from the stress of work is threatened when we take work home with us. Far from being the place where one escapes from domineering bosses, endless email, impending deadlines, and pressures to be more productive, the home instead becomes the locus of these things. To find refuge from work, you now need to find refuge from home, too. Of course, many people have little choice about whether they work from home. And the benefits of doing so can outweigh the costs. But as work takes over your home, the more difficult it is to maintain the home as a refuge from it.

Even when a home offers an escape from the stress of work and politics, it can create stresses of its own. Some homes are chaotic and stressful in their own right. Good homes, though, are peaceful and calm. If you live alone, at minimum you can create a place to pursue hobbies or activities that have nothing to do with work or politics: reading novels, gardening, watching TV. If you live with others, you can create a place that is supportive, encouraging, and loving, irrespective of your job performance or political inclinations.

Home also provides a place to express emotions that are out of place at work, at the coffee shop, or in class. At home you may freely embrace and display deep sadness or romantic passion. After all, not all emotional expressions should be exposed to just anyone. It is good that much of our private lives is concealed and not exposed to the public. As philosopher Thomas Nagel explains, there are two reasons for this.[9] First, private spaces reduce the amount of stuff that must be taken into consideration and responded to by the public. The more stuff exposed in public, the greater chance for disagreement and hostility. Just imagine if everyone's private behaviors and conversations were "out there" in the open, available for public assessment. Concealment therefore has a public function: to buffer against social conflict. Concealment also has a second, private function. Vulnerability and intimacy—whether emotional or physical—require privacy. Private spaces prevent watchful eyes from distorting or destroying valuable activities that require protection from the public gaze. The home, as a stable private place, allows you to express emotions that might otherwise cause public conflicts and creates the very possibility of vulnerability and intimacy.

Finally, home offers a refuge from social life itself. In our public lives, we travel through various social spheres: the sphere of work, politics, religion, and so on. Each sphere has its own distinctive social norms. The social norms at a political rally differ from those at work, and each of those has different social norms from those at church. Since we've already noted how the home offers refuge from work and politics, let's turn our attention to a different realm of public life: the economic sphere.

Most people reading this book participate in a modern market economy. You live in a place with strong private property rights, where labor is specialized and divided across individuals and firms, and where goods and services are typically distributed by way of voluntary transactions guided by the price system. Market institutions have their own norms: seek profit, be honest, negotiate fairly, respect legal property rights, compete with other buyers or other sellers, and so on. These norms make markets work and have greatly improved the material conditions of humanity.

But life is not just one big market. The philosopher G.A. Cohen illustrated this when he asked us to imagine going on a fun camping trip with friends.[10] We bring our cooking pans, coffee, fishing rods, canoes, and decks of cards. We do the activities we enjoy and chip in where we can. What we don't do, Cohen says, is assert our rights over pieces of equipment, renting them out to the highest bidder. We don't trade an hour of hammock time for a piece of fish. We don't charge our friends for the right to use our potato-peeler. We *could* do things this way. But we don't. And one reason we don't is that it's good for there to be aspects of our lives that aren't governed by market norms. The home is such a place, where the norms of "doing business" can be replaced with the norms of family, friendship, and neighborliness. The home can be, to borrow a phrase from Leon Kass, "an assertion against and a recognition of the given dog-eat-dog character of the world."[11]

So far, we've focused on the home as refuge from the public world. But there is another way the home can be a refuge: as an escape from your inner mental life. Time alone with your thoughts is valuable (as we will see in the next chapter). But you also need an escape from your inner mental life to avoid collapsing into rumination and loneliness. We find a refuge from our inner life by opening ourselves up to others. Thankfully, moving outward from the recesses of your mental life need not mean you thrust yourself into the public life of work, politics, or entertainment. Rather, homes provide a middle space for social interaction. They preserve a significant amount of privacy while allowing us to open up socially to roommates, family, and guests. We can now see how, at the same time, home provides a refuge from the private life of the self and a refuge from the public life of society. Homes mediate between the privacy of your inner life and the publicity of your social life.

The point of this section has been to show how good homes are "a refuge from the cruel world of politics and work, an emotional sanctuary."[12] But obviously, not all homes are good ones. For many, the home itself is cruel, a source of abuse, hurt, or loneliness. Growing up in a bad home—one that is not safe, peaceful, or welcoming—is one of the greatest harms one can inflict on a child. Many adults become trapped in bad homes as caretakers or spouses. These pedestrian observations reinforce two points. First, good homes are vital to the mental and physical health of children and adults alike. And second, good homes do not happen automatically. It takes effort and care to create a place of refuge.

HOSPITALITY

For many people, 'hospitality' brings to mind an industry devoted to owning and managing hotels, resorts, restaurants, cruise ships, and theme parks. In fact, you can now go to college and train for a career in hospitality. At my (Brandon's) university, students can get a degree in "Tourism, Hospitality, and Event Management," which prepares graduates for "skilled, innovative, and productive careers" in the field of "hospitality operations."[13] This is not a unique program, even in Ohio (not a part of the country known for its tourism). Just down the road, Ohio State University offers a degree in "hospitality management."[14] There are over 500 colleges and universities that offer such a degree in the United States alone, where hospitality is a $200 billion a year industry.

Perhaps due to the commodification of hospitality as the business of "professionals," we surmise that most readers rarely think about hospitality. You might have friends over for a party, or family over for a holiday dinner. Of course, you try to be a good host. But do you practice *hospitality*? Are you a *hospitable* person? The question itself seems quaint. But this is largely an artifact of modern American culture, which has lost its grip on the importance of hospitality.[15]

One of the first stories in the Bible is about hospitality. It takes place in the Bedouin culture of the ancient Near East. To this day, Bedouins emphasize and practice hospitality in much the same way we find in this passage from the Book of Genesis.[16] Abraham and Sarah welcome three strangers—actually divine messengers—to their tent in the Hebron desert where they have made a home.

> The Lord appeared to Abraham near the great trees of Mamre while he was sitting at the entrance to his tent in the heat of the day. Abraham looked up and saw three men standing nearby. When he saw them, he hurried from the entrance of his tent to meet them and bowed low to the ground. He said, "If I have found favor in your eyes, my lord, do not pass your servant by."[17]

Abraham welcomes the strangers with enthusiasm and humility. He doesn't ask who they are or where they are from—something we will see again in ancient Greek hospitality. Far from being an imposition, Abraham pleads with his guests to do him the honor of hosting them. Abraham continues

> "Let a little water be brought, and then you may all wash your feet and rest under this tree."

Abraham meets the strangers in the searing daytime heat and offers them water to wash and cool their feet and to quench their thirst. He invites them to relax under what tradition has held to be an oak tree.

> "Let me get you something to eat, so you can be refreshed and then go on your way—now that you have come to your servant."
>
> "Very well," they answered, "do as you say."
>
> So Abraham hurried into the tent to Sarah. "Quick," he said, "get three seahs[18] of the flour and knead it and bake some bread."
>
> Then he ran to the herd and selected a choice, tender calf and gave it to a servant, who hurried to prepare it. He then brought some curds and milk and the calf that had been prepared, and set these before them.

Repeatedly we are told Abraham is in a hurry. The norms of Bedouin hospitality stress the importance of demonstrating attentiveness to your guests' needs and comforts. Abraham and Sarah prepare meat and bread soaked in curds and buttermilk, a meal probably very similar to the *mansah* that is still commonly served by Bedouins, and a common dish throughout the Levant.

> While they ate, he stood near them under a tree.

Though it might seem strange or rude, Abraham doesn't share in the meal. Rather, he stands out of the way, ready to serve his guests and meet their needs, a traditional aspect of Bedouin hospitality. Those familiar with this story in Genesis will know that its primary theological significance is not the mere fact that Abraham and Sarah show hospitality, but that they offer it to divine messengers who are about to explain to the very old Abraham and Sarah that in a year they will have a child, thereby fulfilling God's promise to make Abraham a "father of many nations." Even so, Abraham and Sarah's hospitality has throughout the centuries encouraged people to welcome strangers as friends. The New Testament author of Hebrews surely had this story in mind when admonishing the faithful "not [to] forget to show hospitality to strangers, for by so doing some people have shown hospitality to angels without knowing it."[19]

We saw in the previous chapter that Homer's *Odyssey* is one of the great stories of homecoming. But its other great theme is hospitality. Odysseus's long journey home would have been impossible without what the Greeks called *xenia*: friendship of strangers. (Xenia, if you recall, is also the name of the Ohio town destroyed by a tornado we discussed in the last chapter.) The Greek god Zeus was often referred to as Zeus Xenios: the stranger's god. To be inhospitable to guests was an afront to Zeus himself and put one at risk for divine retribution. In ancient Greece, social expectations of hospitality rose to the level of religious obligation. In Book XII of his *Laws*, for example, Plato explains that the Athenians who go abroad should be good guests, and that those who host foreigners should be good hosts: "These are the customs, according to which our city should receive all strangers of either sex who come from other countries, and should send forth her own citizens, showing respect to Zeus, the God of hospitality."[20]

There are no fewer than ten scenes of *xenia* in the *Odyssey*. In the first, the goddess Athena visits the King's son Telemachus in Ithaca, where the King's house has been overrun with suitors vying to marry Queen Penelope. Athena tells the young prince that his father is alive, and he should search for him. He should also banish the suitors who have long overstayed their welcome (a clear case of a guest abusing the host's *xenia*). Athena has taken the form of Odysseus's friend Mentes to disguise her true identity. Upon noticing a guest has arrived, Telemachus wastes no time welcoming the stranger.

> Straight to the porch he went, mortified
> that a guest might still be standing at the doors.
> Pausing beside her there, he clasped her right hand
> and relieving her at once of her long bronze spear,
> met her with winged words: "Greetings, stranger!
> Here in our house you'll find a royal welcome.
> Have supper first, then tell us what you need.[21]

Homeric hospitality rituals follow a predictable pattern. The guest is welcomed and made to feel at home. She is fed and offered drink before any exchanges of identities or information. The host's request for the reason for her visit is secondary to welcoming her and meeting her needs. After Athena has carried her message to Telemachus, he continues the hospitality ritual with the offer of a bath and overnight stay, and then the offer of a gift.

> You've counseled me with so much kindness now,
> like a father to a son. I won't forget a word.
> But come, stay longer, keen as you are to sail,
> so you can bathe and rest and lift your spirits,
> then go back to your ship, delighted with a gift,
> a prize of honor, something rare and fine
> as a keepsake from myself. The kind of gift
> a host will give a stranger, friend to friend.[22]

What is hospitality?

Theologian Henri Nouwen writes that "if there is any concept worth restoring to its original depth and evocative potential, it is the concept of hospitality."[23] But it is not easy to say what hospitality is, and philosophers have written little on the topic.[24]

To begin, it's important to see that hospitality is not the same as charity. You can show charity to total strangers with whom you never interact. You can give money to organizations that help the poor without having a clue who you are helping. Often you don't particularly care who you are helping, as long as some people are helped. Though charitable and perhaps generous, this is not hospitality. Hospitality is not generic giving to unknown persons. We show hospitality to particular people in our lives: neighbors, families, strangers. Furthermore, unlike charity, hospitality requires an act of welcoming. Insofar as it is possible and appropriate, hospitality makes a guest feel at home.

Hospitality is not the mere hosting of guests, however. Owning a bed and breakfast is not hospitality even if, unlike the charitable donor, you exchange emails with your guests to arrange their stay and payment. Hospitality requires a level of attentiveness to your guests, primarily through the recognition and generous meeting of their needs, which requires spending time with them.

Hospitality also goes beyond attentiveness to a guest's needs. A hotel staff member who waits on you hand and foot may be an attentive servant. Hospitality requires more than mere serving. Rather (at least in some cultures) it requires sharing things together—characteristically but not necessarily a meal, drinks, and conversation.

We can say, then, that hospitality is the act of welcoming particular others, meeting their needs, and sharing things together. More simply, hospitality is the activity of *attentive welcoming*.

As an act of welcoming, hospitality offers your guest significant freedom to be themselves in your home. This precludes inviting them to your home to lecture them or correct their political views. You cannot be hospitable while also being a busybody or moralizer. Hospitality allows guests to let their guard down in a foreign place. And most people only feel comfortable doing this when they know they are being accepted, and not treated as someone to be harangued, changed, or judged. To be hospitable you must be prepared to bracket off many differences between you and your guest. Both host and guest suppress disagreements about religion, politics, and moral outlook. This is why it is inappropriate to browbeat your guests with your political views, or to embarrass them by making fun of their voting behavior over a holiday meal. Hospitality means, within very wide limits, giving people freedom to be themselves—the host must set aside many of his own opinions to allow someone to feel free and comfortable. Announcing or imposing your ideas and ways of doing things on guests will suffocate them. Even worse: to ask a guest to leave because of differences of opinion. Hospitality requires acceptance, not hostility.

This acceptance endows hospitality with its transformative power. Hospitality, Henri Nouwen writes, can "convert the *hostis* into a *hospes*, the enemy into a guest."[25] Hospitality can turn strangers into friends. It can make your home a refuge, not just for yourself, but for others. It is remarkable that in the examples of Bedouin and Homeric hospitality we looked at, the hosts welcomed their guests without even asking their identity or business. "Greetings, stranger! … Have supper first, then tell us what you need," Telemachus says. This is a radical kind of acceptance, one that doesn't screen for religion, race, or politics.

Just as a hospitable host must avoid hostility, he must also avoid being overbearing. You have probably had a host who was too friendly, hovering over you, anticipating every conceivable need, or insisting too strongly that you stay longer than you'd like. This is annoying and a violation of *xenia*, which avoids not only hostility but overbearingness. King Menelaus displays this balance in Book XV, when Telemachus leaves in haste after Athena tells him to return to Ithaca.

> I'd never detain you here too long, Telemachus,
> not if your heart is set on going home.
> I'd find fault with another host, I'm sure,
> too warm to his guests, too pressing or too cold.
> Balance is best in all things. It's bad either way,
> spurring the stranger home who wants to linger,
> holding the one who longs to leave—you know,
> 'Welcome the coming, speed the parting guest!'[26]

Home and Hospitality

Homes are the most natural place to show hospitality. Attentive welcoming requires a setting where the host has significant authority and control. You can't welcome someone to a place you have no right to be in the first place (your boss's dining room). You may invite someone to join you in a more public space like a restaurant, bar, or coffee shop, but these places severely restrict your freedom to be generous with your guests: you can't stay late after business hours, you can't just grab a snack off the shelf, you can't offer a shower and shave. It is common to tell guests to "make yourselves at home," something that only makes sense to say when you can make yourself at home.

Homes are prime settings for hospitality also because, as private spaces, they offer a level of comfort that's hard to attain elsewhere. At home you can relax and follow conversation where it leads without worrying about eavesdroppers or interlopers. Guest and host can let their guards down, which is less likely to happen in more public spaces.

Of course, home isn't the only place you can show hospitality. Anywhere you have the right to attentively welcome others can be a place of hospitality. Taxi drivers and store greeters show hospitality in their own way. Teachers extend hospitality to their students in the classroom.[27] But few places match the home as the exemplary setting to welcome guests.

It must be said, however, that not all homes lend themselves to hospitality. No guest wants to stay in a dangerous home. And who enjoys being a guest in a stressful, chaotic home? It is the safe, peaceful, welcoming home that is the most natural setting for hospitality.

These observations may seem so obvious as to be barely worth making. But they must be made explicit to see the connection between hospitality and the home. The main point of this chapter is to help you see that devoting much of your time and resources to creating and maintaining a good home is a morally good investment. One reason a home is a worthwhile investment is because of its unique role as the setting for hospitality. It is good to take the time and effort to create a good home, because that is where hospitality happens.

Few people will deny the value of hospitality, but it may not be immediately obvious why it is worth devoting so much of our energy to it. Some of the reasons for hospitality that motivated ancient people may not appeal to modern readers. While ancient Greeks, Jews, Muslims, and Christians may have thought that any stranger at the door could be an ambassador for the divine, you may find this thought less compelling. Moreover, hospitality for modern readers will often look different than it did in Genesis or the *Odyssey*. Random travelers (divine or not) are unlikely to show up at your home, and even if they did, few would blame you for not inviting them in with a gift and the offer of a bath.

While the mode of or rationale for hospitality may change, hospitality retains its moral significance from age to age and culture to culture. For starters, hospitality forges social bonds. Plato called the connection formed between guest and host *exenothesan*: "ties of hospitality."[28] These ties are formed in several ways. Hospitality makes your home a refuge, not just for yourself, but for others. In offering refuge, you provide a safe and peaceful place for people who don't otherwise have one. Hospitality also converts neighbors from strangers to friends. Many people become very close friends with their neighbors. By opening your home to your neighbors through hospitality, you create local bonds of trust, support, and enjoyment.

Hospitality not only forges social bonds, but it also has the capacity to build bridges, to convert the *hostis* into a *hospes*. Chances are, you have coworkers and neighbors with whom you disagree sharply about religion, politics, or morality. In many contexts of life, these differences bubble up into conflict and hostility. But the norms of hospitality forbid conflict over such matters. Hospitality therefore offers an explicitly prosocial context where strangers can become friends and enjoy each other's company, irrespective of their politics. In a culture where everything from pop music to professional sports to young adult fiction has been thoroughly politicized, contexts where people can be friends and share activities with those across the political divide should be preserved and prized. At the risk of sounding trite, we think that widely practiced hospitality in the home is one of the more promising ways to lower the political temperature and build social trust.[29]

CONCLUSION

Commencement Speech Morality instructs us to act on an abstract love for humanity: save the *world*. Ordinary Morality, on the other hand, teaches us to act on a particular love for actual people in our proximity: invite *your neighbor* to your home for dinner.[30]

7

I have often said that man's unhappiness springs from one thing alone, his incapacity to stay quietly in one room.

Blaise Pascal, *Pensées* 139

ALONE TIME

It's OK to spend a lot of time alone. In solitude, you are not minding anyone else's business. It's the easiest and most obvious way to mind your own. Solitude takes minding your own business to the extreme. If spending a lot of time in solitude is OK, then minding your own business must be OK, too.

However, you will often hear messages that paint solitude in a negative light. One criticism arises from cultural norms that put a premium on interpersonal relationships. What makes life meaningful, say these people, is having many friendships, satisfying romantic love, and an exciting social life. Time spent away from these things is time spent away from what makes life worthwhile.

Another critical message casts solitude as emotionally unhealthy or unpleasant. Spending considerable time alone turns your attention to yourself, which leads to brooding, rumination, and self-reproach. It is no coincidence, these critics attest, that people who are depressed, lonely, or alienated

DOI: 10.4324/9781003459248-7

spend so much time alone. Being alone can also be a painful experience. Solitude is "particularly stressful," write psychologists Christopher Long and James Averill, "for members of technologically advanced societies, who have been trained to believe that aloneness is to be avoided and who therefore are relatively unprepared for its effects."[1]

Commencement Speech Morality also has something critical to say about solitude. Recall from Chapter 1 that this approach to life focuses on finding and righting wrongs in the world and helping others on a grand scale. If these are the right priorities, then solitude distracts from what is really important in life. Political action requires public engagement. Injustice demands outrage and protest. To stand up for what's right, we must make our views known on social media. Time spent in solitude is therefore time stolen from more pressing matters. Perhaps some solitude is necessary for resting and recharging, but you shouldn't take more than you need. You must get back out there.

There is a grain of truth in all these concerns, and we will say more about them later. But to whatever extent people hear these critical messages, many nevertheless choose to spend considerable portions of their lives alone. For some, this amounts to a long daily walk or a weekend retreat. Others spend larger portions of their lives in solitude. They prefer the single life or have personalities well suited to alone time. Others enjoy hobbies that by their nature require long stretches of solitude. Long-haul truckers spend most of their waking hours by themselves. Many monks and hermits live in almost absolute solitude.

Are they wrong to do so? We don't think so, at least not usually. As we explained in Chapter 1, there are many good things in life. As we'll argue in this chapter, solitude affords us the opportunity to pursue many of those things.

A SURPRISING ADVOCATE OF SOLITUDE

The 19th-century British philosopher John Stuart Mill was a prodigious scholar. He wrote about ethical theory, political philosophy, economics, politics, logic, and even poetry. He was also a politician, serving for a short time as a Member of Parliament. He is perhaps best known today for three major contributions. First, in his book *Utilitarianism* (1863), Mill advocated for a theory of morality which says that moral rightness is a matter of doing what produces happiness, and moral wrongness is a matter of doing what produces unhappiness. According to Mill, morality is about doing things with good consequences, and we should try to do things that produce the most happiness for the most people.

In some circles, Mill is most famous for his book *On Liberty* (1859), perhaps the single most important defense of the liberal idea that individuals have a right to live their lives as they see fit, so long as they aren't violating others' rights. Mill is especially concerned to defend the right to express one's opinions, free from both censorship from the government and social sanction from other citizens. Mill thought we would live happier lives and that society could make progress if people were allowed a robust freedom to speak their minds.

Finally, Mill is known for his interest in moral and social reform. He sought to change laws and customs to increase overall happiness in society. As a Member of Parliament, and with his wife Harriet Taylor Mill, he worked to promote social progress by opposing slavery and defending women's suffrage. He laid out these arguments in his essay *The Subjugation of Women* (1869).

Given Mill's interest in increasing societal happiness, the value he places on the free exchange of ideas, and his devotion to moral and social progress, you might expect him to be an enthusiastic advocate for Commencement Speech Morality, admonishing us to get out there and change the world. One might easily imagine Mill encouraging us to exercise our right to free expression to use social media to convince others of the path toward social progress and happy lives. Mill's utilitarian outlook is perhaps the one most commonly invoked by those who mind others' business and try to change the world.

It might be surprising to learn, then, that Mill felt strongly about the value of solitude. In fact, Mill thought that spending considerable time in solitude was a crucial ingredient of a good life. In his book *Principles of Political Economy*, published in 1848, Mill wrote:

> It is not good for man to be kept perforce at all times in the presence of his species. A world from which solitude is extirpated is a very poor ideal. Solitude, in the sense of being often alone, is essential to any depth of meditation or of character; and solitude in the presence of natural beauty and grandeur, is the cradle of thoughts and aspirations which are not only good for the individual, but which society could ill do without.[2]

Here we find the most famous utilitarian, and one of the most progressive moral reformers of his day, arguing that minding your own business in the form of extended solitude is good not only for you, but for your society. Why? Mill hints at his reasons for so highly prizing solitude: it helps improve your thinking, character, and creativity. We will return shortly to a defense of solitude, but we first need a better grasp of what it is.

WHAT IS SOLITUDE?

Solitude is the experience of social disengagement.[3] In solitude we do not interact with other humans, and they make no immediate demands on us. Solitude is standing on a secluded riverbank to fish. Solitude is sitting in your favorite chair in the quiet of the night reading a book. It is an open-ended experience that can be accompanied by a great diversity of activities. It can also involve doing nothing much at all. What is crucial to this notion of disengaged solitude is that our experience is characterized by what is missing: social interaction with other people.

Solitude comes in degrees. In extreme solitude, you're not observing or being observed by anyone. You are also physically distant from them. You do not dwell on thoughts of other people or long for them. Instead, your mind is focused on your surroundings and your attention is devoted to whatever activity you're involved in.

But there are also instances of solitude where the social disengagement isn't so extreme. While hiking alone, you might be aware that others glimpse you and you them, even if you have no interaction. You may put down your book to think of a friend you miss. While its boundaries are unclear, the heart of solitude is the relative lack of social engagement with other humans.

Our experiences of solitude also vary in length. Some solitude is episodic, such as when you lay in bed at night, alone in the stillness. You might find a short period of solitude cooking dinner for yourself at home, going for a long evening walk beside cornfields, practicing piano, smoking a cigar by the fireplace, or any number of other activities. Some solitude lasts longer, like when you spend a rainy weekend listening to music, reading, and cleaning your apartment. Some people go on personal retreats and spend a week or more in almost total solitude. And, as we already noted, some people voluntarily spend much of their adult lives in relative solitude.

We're interested in the notion of solitude as an experience of social disengagement. But people do commonly use the term in different ways. In his book *A History of Solitude*, historian David Vincent identifies these other senses, and by briefly discussing them, we can clarify the notion of disengaged solitude we have in mind here.

Sometimes "solitude" refers to *physical solitude*: being physically distant from others.[4] You could hole up, for example, in a secluded cabin in search of this kind of solitude. However, physical solitude is often but not always accompanied by socially disengaged solitude. Modern technology allows you to spend an entire weekend in a remote cabin all the while staying in constant communication with others. You could even exhaust yourself from this sort of social interaction, all the while remaining miles from anyone else.[5]

There is another sense of solitude, one that involves, not physical distance, but psychological distance. Sometimes we have the experience of "tuning out" what is happening around us and "being in our own world." We focus on our natural surroundings, like a sunset, or on our own thoughts, like when we try to figure out how to handle a difficult work situation. In this kind of *abstracted solitude* you feel alone even though you are physically close to others. You may have had an experience of "being in your own world" while listening to music at the gym or reading on a plane.

These are perfectly fine senses of solitude with which we have no issue. But here we'll focus on solitude as an experience of social disengagement because it's the form of solitude that most clearly involves minding your own business. Even in physical solitude, for instance, you can still stick your nose into others' business. The Internet provides endless opportunities to moralize about others' behavior or meddle in their affairs. And in abstracted solitude, while you might be "in your own headspace," you are still physically near others, who may be observing you, evaluating you. They can still make immediate demands upon you, and you upon them. And in the blink of an eye, you can be jerked back into social interaction.

Solitude comes in degrees and the distinctions between various forms of solitude are fuzzy. Nevertheless, the idea of disengaged solitude will help us see why it's okay to mind your own business. Before turning to what can be said in defense of solitude, however, we must first distinguish it from two other kinds of experiences.

Understandably, solitude is often associated with loneliness. Loneliness evokes images of the solitary retiree eating microwave dinners and watching television re-runs, or perhaps the child forced to sit by herself at lunch because no one wants to be her friend. It's true of course that lonely people often spend much of their time in solitude, often not by choice. But it's important to recognize that solitude and loneliness are distinct.

Loneliness is the unpleasant feeling of longing for social engagement.[6] Typically, we feel lonely because we long for *any* positive social interaction, a defining experience of shut-ins, many elderly, and prisoners who spend long stretches in solitary confinement.

But solitude is not the same thing as loneliness. For starters, you can feel lonely when you aren't in solitude. Attending your sixth wedding this summer without a date, you might feel terribly lonely as a single person, even as you dance in the crowd at a reception party. But the reverse is true, as well: you can experience solitude without feeling lonely. Many people feel wholly content and joyful in their own company, absorbed in some activity, even for long periods of time. As Christopher Long and James Averill explain, "In contrast to loneliness, which by definition involves a negative emotional script, solitude is a more open-ended experience."[7] As we will see, this open-endedness of solitude is one of the keys to seeing why solitude can be so valuable.

We should also distinguish solitude from alienation. Now throughout the centuries, philosophers of diverse stripes have used the term "alienation" to refer to many different things.[8] Karl Marx, for example, used the notion of alienation (or "estrangement") to describe the effect that capitalist economic arrangements have on workers. Capitalism, he thought, breaks down the wholeness of a person and her relations with other workers.

The sense of alienation that concerns us here, however, owes itself to the early 19th century German philosopher G.W.F. Hegel. Sometimes we don't feel at home in the world, Hegel pointed out, an experience we understand as early as adolescence. We feel foreign to others, to places we inhabit, or perhaps even to ourselves. We feel like we don't belong. Much has been written about this sense of alienation and we won't rehearse that literature here. The main point is just that the need to feel at home in the world is a very important one, and when that need is not met, people will tend to feel alienated.

Alienation and solitude share common ground, for in each you might feel that you are "on your own" in the world. Yet, while solitude and alienation might accompany one another, they should be clearly distinguished. Much like loneliness, you can feel alienated in a crowd. And alienation, like loneliness, has a negative emotional script. Whereas loneliness is characterized by a longing for interaction, however, the heart of alienation is a longing to belong. Solitude, however, as we have already seen, is a more open-ended emotional experience: there's nothing about solitude that requires either one of these negative feelings. In fact, as we will see, solitude can aid us in our search for attachments. Far from being alienating, solitude can be the very thing that helps us feel at home in the world.

IN DEFENSE OF SOLITUDE

What can be said in favor of solitude? We think a lot—much more than can be detailed in this short book.[9] But what we do say in its defense shows that there are many important things in life that are best (or only) attained through solitude.

It's fair to ask how much solitude is OK. On the one hand, we suspect most readers already agree with us that it's permissible to spend small portions of their day in solitude, minding their own business. Minimally, then, there's nothing wrong with spending small amounts of time by yourself. This will seem like common sense. Even so, it's worthwhile to see why solitude is part of a morally good life.

However, Commencement Speech Morality can lead us to think that anything more than minimal solitude is morally suspect. Solitude is selfish when there are so many problems in the world to solve. We may feel guilty about privileging our own personal business over the immediate interests and needs of others, even those of our friends and family. In our view, the virtues of solitude justify considerable time spent alone, at least for many of us. This is clear when we recognize that, for many people, the demands of work and family leave little time for solitude, and that the virtues of solitude can only be attained in the time left over. But we think the value of solitude is such that even large amounts of it are consistent with living a morally good life. It's OK for world class swimmers to spend hours a day in solitude swimming laps. It's OK for people seeking spiritual enlightenment to live more or less as hermits. We don't have a way of determining exactly how much solitude is OK for you, and we are suspicious of any philosopher who would try to tell you otherwise.

One more point: as we mentioned, not all solitude is chosen. Some solitude is enforced, as in the case of prisoners. Some solitude is non-voluntary, a common experience of shut-ins. Although many of the virtues of solitude we discuss can be had in enforced and non-voluntary solitude, we will focus on solitude that is voluntarily chosen. In our view, the virtues of solitude are most apparent when the experience is voluntary. Furthermore, since we think of solitude as one way to mind your own business, and will argue that it's OK to mind your own business, our defense of solitude naturally falls to its voluntary instances. It's OK to choose solitude, or so we will argue.

Rest

Humans have a deep and abiding desire for social interaction and community.[10] But living in constant communion with others can be tiring and stressful. Solitude gives us the opportunity to rest. Rest is good not merely because we need it to carry on with further social interactions, though of course it does serve that purpose. Rather, rest is also good in its own right.[11]

Solitude provides a space that is free from the stresses of social life. When we interact with others, we're aware of how we look, our posture, the sound of our voice, the words we're saying, and most generally, the fact that we are being observed at all. We in turn watch others to learn the relevant norms and expectations for how we should behave, to identify violations of morality or etiquette, and to defend ourselves against accusations that we have violated them.

Solitude, however, relieves us from the task of what psychologists call "impression management," our method of controlling how others perceive us.[12] Much social interaction requires, at some level of awareness, that we monitor and manage the impressions we give off to others, about how attractive, or funny, or smart, or moral we are. Even in large crowds where you might feel anonymous and thus let down your guard, there is still pressure to fit in.[13]

Life with others can also be stressful because of our awareness of the social status hierarchy, and the efforts we all make to improve our rank in it.[14] We become aware that others are funnier, more attractive, or smarter. This constant social comparison can be a source of stress, and even conflict. Nineteenth-century English poet John Clare correctly identified the antidote, though: "O thou soothing Solitude, / From the vain and from the rude."[15]

Although solitude is a little-studied topic in psychology, there is some evidence that people pursue the restfulness of solitude precisely because it allows us to escape the stresses of social life. In 2016, BBC journalist Claudia Hammond partnered with psychiatric researcher Gemma Lewis and an interdisciplinary team of experts to conduct the largest-ever survey about how people think about rest.[16] More than 18,000 people from 134 countries were given a list of 25 activities and asked to list the three most restful. Here were the top ten:

1. Reading
2. Sleeping or napping
3. Looking at, or being in, a natural environment
4. Spending time on my own
5. Listening to music
6. Doing nothing in particular
7. Walking
8. Taking a bath or shower
9. Daydreaming
10. Watching TV

As Hammond herself observes, all these activities are often done alone (especially number 4!). Introverts and extroverts alike tended to rank these solitary activities ahead of more social activities like spending time with friends and family, chatting, and social drinking. People seem to find something particularly restful in solitude, perhaps because solitude blunts the stress of impression management and the pressure to navigate the social hierarchy.

An additional explanation might be the role solitude can play in regulating our emotions. Recent studies suggest that solitude can promote relaxation and reduce stress by deactivating "high-arousal" feelings, whether they are positive (such as feeling excited, enthusiastic, inspired) or negative (feeling upset, afraid, hostile).[17]

Solitude is a valuable part of life, and not simply because it refreshes us to get back out there to right wrongs and help others more effectively. It is good in itself to rest from the stresses of social life.

Freedom

One often-observed benefit of solitude is freedom.[18] Psychologists Christopher Long and James Averill even characterize solitude itself as, in part, "a state of reduced social inhibition and increased freedom to select one's mental or physical activities."[19] In solitude we can think as we like. We are free to engage in activities at our own pace, and are under no immediate demands from others to do them in a certain way. The famous 19th-century British essayist and literary critic William Hazlitt thought this kind of freedom was attainable only in solitude, and especially when going for a walk.

> The soul of a [solitary] journey is liberty, perfect liberty, to think, feel, do, just as one pleases ... I want to see my

vague notions float like the down of the thistle before the breeze, and not to have them entangled in the briars and thorns of controversy. For once, I like to have it all my own way; and this is impossible unless you are alone.[20]

Of course, for freedom to be good in this way, we need not think that just *anything* we do in solitude is valuable. As 19th-century poet Matthew Arnold remarked, freedom is "a very good horse to ride, but to ride somewhere."[21]

We agree that there is significant value in this freedom of thought and action provided by solitude, but we want to return to John Stuart Mill and focus on a certain kind of freedom he thought was only attained through solitude: intellectual freedom.[22]

Mill is famous for his defense of the right to express our opinions, free from both legal interference and social pressure. He thinks that, in the long run, it's better from the perspective of overall societal happiness to allow for a wide manner of speech. He also thought that putting limits on speech, even limits on saying things that are false or offensive, makes it harder not only to arrive at the truth, but to remember why we believe the truths of which we are in possession.

However, Mill did not think that the free exchange of ideas was a guarantee that deliberation and conversation would ultimately land on moral or political truth. Mill would not be at all surprised, for instance, that so many discussions on social media lead us away from the truth, not toward it.

> I have not any great notion of the advantage of what the "free discussion" men, call the "collision of opinions", it being my creed that Truth is sown and germinates in the mind itself, and is not to be struck out suddenly like fire from a flint by knocking another hard body against it.[23]

The setting in which truth is sown and germinated in the mind is, according to Mill, solitude. For in solitude, we "let the feelings of society cease to stigmatize independent thinking."[24] And here we see Mill's primary concern about effects of social interaction and public discourse on the life of the mind: it tends to turn us into conformists. Independent thinkers must step outside their society to obtain a critical distance from it and be free from the pressures that society imposes on those who criticize it. "To most people," Mill wrote, "society is a relaxation; we, on the contrary, need relaxation from society; & to pass half our time in the virtual solitude in which we live here is not merely a luxury but a necessity to us."[25] The "we" that Mill has in mind here primarily refers to writers, philosophers, and poets. To do their work, they need the requisite distance from society to see its faults and to tell the hard truths without fear. Solitude, Mill thought, provided the necessary space to exercise intellectual freedom.

Mill thought that people like philosophers are the most in need of the intellectual benefits of solitude. But we think his concern about intellectual conformism applies to all of us who aspire to think critically about what goes on in our culture. As important as community is for creatures like us, Mill recognized that society can have a deadening effect on the mind. Without the space to step back and critically assess what we hear and see from friends and strangers, humans are liable to go with the flow, accepting what our friends think, or rejecting what our enemies think. One of the more depressing discoveries in psychology of the past half-century is just how prone we are to groupthink, uncritically accepting the beliefs of our peers.[26] But if Mill is right, solitude can help us think for ourselves, away from the immediate pressure to conform.

Just after completing *On Liberty*, Mill wrote in a letter "that those who would either make their lives useful to noble ends, or maintain any elevation of character within themselves, must in these days have little to do with what is called society."[27] Perhaps this overstates the case. But a considerable amount of solitude may be the best opportunity you have to develop an independent mind, one capable of critically and fairly assessing your culture.

Appreciation and Achievement

If you were to pause and think of your life—about how you spend your time and what occupies your thoughts—you'd likely find that much of it is directed at other people. We eat meals with others, text our friends, date, shop amidst huge crowds, and sit in coffee shops.

But some valuable aspects of life don't involve other people. Activities are not worthwhile merely because they involve social interaction or because you are meeting someone else's wants or needs. Solitude allows us to appreciate these nonpersonal aspects of life. We'll briefly mention two such aspects.

The first is the enjoyment and appreciation of impersonal nature. It is good to enjoy the beauty of our natural environs, to delight in the midnight stars off the coast of Andros Island. Of course, such things can be enjoyed with others. But they need not be. And there is nothing wrong with appreciating such things on our own. Or with a dog. As we've been thinking of solitude, it's an experience characterized by a lack of social interaction with other humans. Who would argue that spending time with a beloved dog is not OK?

Solitude also makes possible so much human greatness. Not all human achievements require solitude, or much solitude anyway. But many do. Probably more than you think.

Being a world class swimmer requires endless hours alone in a pool. The world's best mathematicians have spent uncountable hours alone trying to solve problems. Poets and writers for hundreds of years have sat alone and stared at blank sheets of paper. Does Puccini write "Nessun Dorma" without solitude? Does Michelangelo sculpt David? Do NASA mathematicians take photographs of Saturn? But you don't need to be capable of world-class human achievements or acts of great creativity to use solitude productively.[28] Your daily piano practicing is a valuable human achievement. So is the painting or woodworking you do on the weekends. In solitude we are able to focus completely on healthy and enjoyable activities that are worth our time and attention.

IS SOLITUDE SELFISH?

Like anything else in life, you can have too much of a good thing. Solitude is no different. For most of us, it's OK to spend time in solitude, even in considerable amounts. Many people do spend time in solitude, and it's probably OK for them to spend more time alone than they currently do. There are many good things about living, and as we've tried to show, some are best done in solitude. Others are only possible in solitude.

We haven't argued that solitude is morally obligatory. And for some of us, spending much time in solitude might be morally wrong. People vary in temperament in ways that can make extended periods of solitude unhealthy and counterproductive. Some of us have certain obstacles or challenges that would be exacerbated by time alone. Others have, for one reason or another, constant demands on their time and energy from close friends or family. In all these situations we have no interest in trying to force solitude onto people. For this reason you might think that our goal of showing it's OK to spend a considerable portion of your life in solitude is a low bar. We agree. After all, this book has been a defense of the way many people already live their lives. We aren't trying to defend anything radical.

According to the critic of solitude, however, spending considerable time alone is selfish. Perhaps it's OK to spend whatever time alone that you need to be happy and healthy. But beyond that, you are stealing from others in great need. Or maybe it's OK to spend more time in solitude than is strictly necessary for your health and happiness, but in doing so, you should be doing things that still help others. If you want to spend lots of time alone, that's OK, you just need to quilt blankets for the homeless.

As we'll explain, we don't think considerable solitude is necessarily selfish. We don't expect to convince the dyed-in-the-wool Commencement Speech Moralists. But if you're inclined to Ordinary Morality and worry that solitude seems unduly self-centered, there is no reason for worry.

Why might solitude be selfish? Perhaps it is because solitude robs others of the opportunity to see good people and good behavior. When good people hide, they remove positive role models from social view. Enlightenment philosopher Denis Diderot raised this exact objection against the religious monks and hermits who lived mostly outside mainstream society:

> A truly robust virtue is one that walks firmly through obstacles, and not one that flees them ... A solitary is, in regard to the rest of mankind, like an inanimate being; his prayers and his contemplative life, which no one sees, have no influence on society which has more need of examples of virtue before its eyes than in the forests.[29]

To respond, first, it's possible to have a positive influence on society without setting a public example. You could do conservation work without making a big stink about it, or anonymously drop off your home-made quilts at the local homeless shelter. So Diderot is mistaken to claim that solitaries have no influence on society.

Even so, Diderot might contend that virtuous people have an obligation to show others their virtue. Maybe, but at best this could only be plausibly construed as an obligation that *sometimes, some people* should be able to see you act out your virtue. And most of us, save only the most solitary hermit, meet that obligation.

Even if Diderot were correct that the spiritually and morally enlightened among us have a duty to be seen performing their virtue in public, it's less clear that the rest of us have the same duty. Though we tend to the think we are morally better than the average person, most of us are, morally speaking, a mixed bag.[30] People like us do good things in public, but we also do bad things. So even if those of "robust virtue" have a duty to be seen doing good in public, this does not mean the rest of us also have the same duty.

A second way you might think solitude is selfish is the most obvious one: when in solitude we deprive others of the help we could be giving them. And there are certainly many pressing needs in the world, needs that you could be meeting instead of reading this book. Certainly, there are people in our lives who depend on us to provide for them, keep them safe, and fulfill our duties. But there is a danger in thinking of ourselves primarily in terms of our usefulness to others. We are not merely useful to others, nor are they to us. Sometimes we must be *useless* to others. This uselessness to others itself has its own kind of utility, as the benefits of solitude show.

"We don't become lovable objects," explains philosopher Roger Scruton, "by becoming useful, although we should lend our help to others and so on. We become lovable by enjoying the world and radiating our appreciation of it."[31] Solitude allows us, above all, to be lovable.

CONCLUSION

Even if you've come to see the virtues of minding your own business, you may still feel that a life devoted to rootedness, home life, and solitude is missing something desirable. For what Commencement Speech Morality promises (even if it doesn't always deliver) is notoriety, fame, reputation, and glory. If you do great things on a big enough stage, you can be famous. By appealing to our self-love, the Commencement Speech Moralist moves us to tackle the world's problems, for there's something in it for us. The life of minding your business, on the other hand, promises not fame but obscurity, and on this promise it will deliver. And who wants to be a nobody living in obscurity? Understandable as it is, though, this way of thinking is mistaken, too. The error, as Epictetus recognized, is in thinking you can't be a somebody in those small areas of life where you might make the biggest difference. "How can you be a 'nobody in obscurity,' " he asks, "when you only have to be somebody in the areas you control—the areas, that is, where you have the ability to shine?"[32]

Epilogue

Is This Water?

Throughout this book, we have criticized commencement speeches for imparting to young people a distorted moral vision, one that tells them to get out there and do big things to change the world. But not all commencement speeches preach this message.

In 2005, novelist David Foster Wallace addressed the graduates at Kenyon College with the now-famous "This Is Water" speech. He began:

> There are these two young fish swimming along and they happen to meet an older fish swimming the other way, who nods at them and says, "Morning, boys. How's the water?" And the two young fish swim on for a bit, and then eventually one of them looks over at the other and goes, "What the hell is water?"[1]

Wallace continued:

> The immediate point of the fish story is merely that the most obvious, ubiquitous, important realities are often the ones that are hardest to see and talk about. Stated as an English sentence, of course, this is just a banal platitude—but the fact is that, in the day-to-day trenches of adult existence, banal platitudes can have a life-or-death

DOI: 10.4324/9781003459248-X

importance. Or so I wish to suggest to you on this dry and lovely morning.[2]

You might think much of this book has been banal platitudes: it's dangerous to mind others' business, it's admirable to mind your own, put down roots, build a good home, spend time in solitude. Did we really need a whole book to tell you these things? Is this water?

It's true we've defended the commonplace, the traditional, the low-profile life. If these things are banal, our reply, with Wallace, is that such truths sometimes need to be said. It's easy to be drawn to the novel, the radical, the surprising, and there is no shortage of voices preaching such a life. Indeed, a central expectation of academic philosophy is that philosophers should defend the unexpected and unconventional rather than what is banal and commonplace. We hope to have spoken up for the banal truth right in front of you.

Notes

1

1 www.oberlin.edu/news/transcript-first-lady-michelle-obamas-commencement-address [accessed 4/1/20].

2 https://time.com/3882613/bill-nye-graduation-speech-rutgers-university/ [accessed 4/1/20].

3 https://time.com/collection-post/3882654/katie-couric-graduation-speech-2015/ [accessed 4/1/20].

4 https://time.com/collection-post/3889267/salman-rushdie-graduation-speech-emory/ [accessed 4/1/20].

5 In 2017, Kent State University paid actress Octavia Spencer $100,000 for her 20-minute commencement speech. (www.cleveland.com/metro/2017/04/kent_state_to_pay_100000_for_o.html [accessed 11/7/2022]. In 2006, the University of Oklahoma paid journalist Katie Couric $110,000, and the University of Houston dished out $135,000 to actor Matthew McConaughey in 2015. www.insidehighered.com/news/2015/04/02/matthew-mcconaugheys-pricey-commencement-speaker-fee-not-out-norm [accessed 11/7/2022].

6 Charles Dickens, *A Christmas Carol and Other Stories* (New York: Modern Library, 2001), 13.

7 For a rare defense of Scrooge, see Gerald Gaus, "On the Difficult Virtue of Minding One's Own Business: Towards the Political Rehabilitation of Ebenezer Scrooge," *The Philosopher: A Magazine for Free Spirits* 5 (1997): 24–28.

8 Dickens, *A Christmas Carol and Other Stories*, 25.

9 Thucydides, *History of the Peloponnesian War*, trans. Rex Warner, Revised Edition (Harmondsworth, UK: Penguin Classics, 1972), para. 2.40.

10 Sinclair Lewis, *It Can't Happen Here*, Reprint edition (New York: Signet, 2014), 117.

11 John Stuart Mill, *Essays On Ethics, Religion And Society* (Indianapolis, IN: Liberty Fund Inc., 2006), 94.

12 www.givewell.org/charities/malaria-consortium [accessed 4/2/20].

13 According to GiveWell, it costs Malaria Consortium about $2300 to save a life. So even if you contribute just a fraction of that amount, you're doing a lot of good. www.givewell.org/giving101/Your-dollar-goes-further-overseas [accessed 4/2/20].

14 This simple statement of the theory glosses over many difficult issues that need not detain us here. For more about utilitarianism and related moral theories, see: https://plato.stanford.edu/entries/consequentialism/ [accessed 4/3/20].

15 The picture of Ordinary Morality just described is inspired by W. D. Ross's pluralistic moral theory. In some ways, it departs from Ross's stated view. But we admire Ross's theory in part for coming the closest of all moral theories we're aware of to capturing how ordinary people actually reason when they think about moral decisions. See David Ross, *The Right and the Good* (New York: Oxford University Press, 2002).

2

1 Julia Driver, "Moralism," *Journal of Applied Philosophy* 22, no. 2 (2005): 137, https://doi.org/10.1111/j.1468-5930.2005.00298.x.

2 Driver, 138.

3 Driver, 148.

4 As Driver notices, 150n6. We think this is a challenge to any account of moralizing, including our own.

5 This isn't to say that it's no vice to have extremely demanding judgments that you don't act on, but that is a different kind of moral flaw that we won't discuss here.

6 Philosophers have explored many ways of identifying the moral demands we should enforce through social or political coercion. We won't propose a full account here beyond the limits discussed in this section. For our purposes, it's enough to say that moralizers' ambitions for social enforcement exceed the limits of the correct account of social morality. That is what makes them moralizers. For some popular accounts, see: John Stuart Mill, *On Liberty and Other Writings* (Cambridge: Cambridge University Press, 1989); P. F. Strawson, "Social Morality and Individual Ideal," *Philosophy* 36, no. 136 (1961): 1–17; Gerald Gaus,

Why It's OK to Mind Your Own Business

The Order of Public Reason: A Theory of Freedom and Morality in a Diverse and Bounded World (New York: Cambridge University Press, 2011).

7   For a helpful discussion of roles and moralizing, see Robert K. Fullinwider, "On Moralism," *Journal of Applied Philosophy* 22, no. 2 (2005): 105–20.

8   Our discussion of these considerations is inspired by Jeanette Bicknell's helpful account of sanctimonious self-righteousness. See Jeanette Bicknell, "Self-Righteousness as a Moral Problem," *The Journal of Value Inquiry* 44, no. 4 (2010): 477–87, https://doi.org/10.1007/s10790-010-9247-8.

9   For more on such standing see, for example, Patrick Todd, "A Unified Account of the Moral Standing to Blame," *Noûs* 53, no. 2 (2019): 347–74, https://doi.org/10.1111/nous.12215; Kyle G. Fritz and Daniel J. Miller, "A Standing Asymmetry between Blame and Forgiveness," *Ethics* 132, no. 4 (2022): 759–86, https://doi.org/10.1086/719511.

10 Ross, *The Right and the Good*, 21.

11 We have in mind generally those moral philosophers who make the demands of morality an integral and overriding element of practical reason. The clearest case is the strand of Kantian thought—influenced by Rousseau's claim that we can force people to be free because the general will is their true will—that treats moral action as free action, so that morality cannot be a limit on freedom. See https://plato.stanford.edu/entries/kant-moral/ [accessed 12/7/22]. "At the heart of Kant's moral theory is the idea of autonomy. Most readers interpret Kant as holding that autonomy is a property of rational wills or agents. Understanding the idea of autonomy was, in Kant's view, key to understanding and justifying the authority that moral requirements have over us. As with Rousseau, whose views influenced Kant, freedom does not consist in being bound by no law, but by laws that are in some sense of one's own making."

12 Bernard Williams, *Ethics and the Limits of Philosophy* (Cambridge, MA: Harvard University Press, 1986), 192.

13 Think, for instance, of the norm that the closeness of your relationship limits the kind of advice you should offer someone. It's one thing to tell your spouse to get off Twitter and touch grass. It's another thing entirely to say this to the Jacob Urowsky Professor of Philosophy at Yale University.

14 Bicknell, "Self-Righteousness as a Moral Problem," 479–82. The episode is described in greater detail here: www.theglobeandmail.com/news/national/the-bra-haha-that-went-global/article975867/ [accessed 6/9/20].

15 Jessica Kennedy and Maurice E. Schweitzer, "Holding People Responsible for Ethical Violations: The Surprising Benefits of Accusing Others," *Academy of Management Proceedings* 2015, no. 1 (2015): 112–58, https://doi.org/10.5465/ambpp.2015.11258abstract.

16 "With their virtue they want to scratch out the eyes of their enemies, and they exalt themselves only to humble others." Friedrich Nietzsche, *Thus Spoke Zarathustra: A Book for All and None*, trans. Walter Kaufmann (New York: Modern Library, 1995), 95.

17 Fullinwider, "On Moralism," 110.

18 Philosopher Nathan Ballantyne calls the phenomenon of experts attempting to exert influence outside of their actual area of expertise "epistemic trespassing." See Nathan Ballantyne, "Epistemic Trespassing," *Mind* 128, no. 510 (2019): 367–95, https://doi.org/10.1093/mind/fzx042.

19 Robert Nozick, *Anarchy, State, and Utopia* (New York: Basic Books, 1974), 247.

20 www.washingtonpost.com/politics/2019/01/07/alexandria-ocasio-cortezs-very-bad-defense-her-falsehoods/ [accessed 12/6/22].

21 According to rent control advocacy group Tenants Together, for instance, limits on increases in rent are "a matter of basic fairness." https://www.tenantstogether.org/campaigns/rent-control-all [accessed 6/11/20].

22 Richard M. Alston, J. R. Kearl, and Michael B. Vaughan, "Is There a Consensus Among Economists in the 1990's?," *The American Economic Review* 82, no. 2 (1992): 204. In a survey of over 400 Canadian economists, 95 percent agreed with the statement. Walter Block and Michael Walker, "Entropy in the Canadian Economics Profession: Sampling Consensus on the Major Issues," *Canadian Public Policy / Analyse de Politiques* 14, no. 2 (1988): 143–44, https://doi.org/10.2307/3550573.

23 Julia Driver, "Hyperactive Ethics," *The Philosophical Quarterly* 44, no. 174 (1994): 23, https://doi.org/10.2307/2220144

24 Justin Tosi and Brandon Warmke, *Grandstanding: The Use and Abuse of Moral Talk* (New York: Oxford University Press, 2020), 85–88.

25 Nico H. Frijda, *The Laws of Emotion* (Mahwah, NJ: Psychology Press, 2006), 10–11; Seymour Epstein, "Expectancy and Magnitude of Reaction to a

Noxious UCS," *Psychophysiology* 10, no. 1 (1973): 100–107, https://doi.org/10.1111/j.1469-8986.1973.tb01091.x; Frances K. McSweeney and Samantha Swindell, "General-Process Theories of Motivation Revisited: The Role of Habituation," *Psychological Bulletin* 125, no. 4 (1999): 437.

26 David L. Dickinson and David Masclet, "Emotion Venting and Punishment in Public Good Experiments," *Journal of Public Economics* 122 (February 1, 2015): 55–67, https://doi.org/10.1016/j.jpubeco.2014.10.008.

3

1 Theophrastus, *The Characters of Theophrastus*, trans. Isaac Taylor (London: A.J. Valpy, 1831), 36–37.

2 Plutarch, *Moralia*, trans. William Clark Helmbold, vol. 6, Loeb Classical Library 337 (Cambridge, MA: Harvard University Press, 1939), 483.

3 "If you suffer, it should not be as a murderer or thief or any other kind of criminal, or even as a meddler" (1 Peter 4:15 NIV). The King James Version translates *allotriepiskopos* as "busybody." For discussion see Jeannine K. Brown, "Just a Busybody? A Look at the Greco-Roman Topos of Meddling for Defining *allotriepiskopos* in 1 Peter 4:15," *Journal of Biblical Literature* 125, no. 3 (2006): 549–68, https://doi.org/10.2307/27638379.

4 To be more precise, it's an inappropriate *attempted* exercise of helping behavior, since the busybody need not actually help anyone even though they try. But this shorthand is fine.

5 Epictetus, *Discourses, Books 3–4. Fragments. The Encheiridion*, trans. W. A. Oldfather, Loeb Classical Library 218 (Cambridge, MA: Harvard University Press, 1928), 165–67.

6 Plutarch, *Moralia*, 6:473–517.

7 Plutarch, 6:475.

8 Peter Singer, "Famine, Affluence, and Morality," *Philosophy & Public Affairs* 1, no. 3 (1972): 231.

9 www.aidforafrica.org/girls/how-much-does-school-cost/ [accessed 8/20/20].

10 Thomas Taylor, trans., *Political Fragments of Archytas, Charondas, Zaleucus, and Other Ancient Pythagoreans, Preserved by Stobaeus, and Also, Ethical Fragments of Hierocles* (Walworth, UK: Printed by C. Whittingham for the translator, 1822), 106–9.

11 See, e.g., Peter Singer, *The Expanding Circle: Ethics, Evolution, and Moral Progress*, Revised (Princeton, NJ: Princeton University Press, 2011); Americus

Reed II and Karl F. Aquino, "Moral Identity and the Expanding Circle of Moral Regard toward Out-Groups," *Journal of Personality and Social Psychology* 84 (2003): 1270–86, https://doi.org/10.1037/0022-3514.84.6.1270; Boyka Bratanova, Steve Loughnan, and Birgitta Gatersleben, "The Moral Circle as a Common Motivational Cause of Cross-Situational pro-Environmentalism," *European Journal of Social Psychology* 42, no. 5 (2012): 539–45, https://doi.org/10.1002/ejsp.1871; Simon M. Laham, "Expanding the Moral Circle: Inclusion and Exclusion Mindsets and the Circle of Moral Regard," *Journal of Experimental Social Psychology* 45, no. 1 (2009): 250–53, https://doi.org/10.1016/j.jesp.2008.08.012; Jacy Reese Anthis and Eze Paez, "Moral Circle Expansion: A Promising Strategy to Impact the Far Future," *Futures* 130 (2021): 102756, https://doi.org/10.1016/j.futures.2021.102756.

12 "Those who have many friends and mix intimately with them all are thought to be no one's friend." Aristotle, *The Complete Works of Aristotle: The Revised Oxford Translation*, ed. Jonathan Barnes, Revised Edition, vol. 2 (Princeton, NJ: Princeton University Press, 1984), 150.

13 Charles R. Figley, "Compassion Fatigue as Secondary Traumatic Stress Disorder: An Overview," in *Compassion Fatigue: Coping with Secondary Stress Disorder in Those Who Treat the Traumatised*, ed. Charles R. Figley (Bristol, UK: Brunner/Mazel, 1995).

14 Katherine N. Kinnick, Dean M. Krugman, and Glen T. Cameron, "Compassion Fatigue: Communication and Burnout toward Social Problems," *Journalism & Mass Communication Quarterly* 73, no. 3 (1996): 697, https://doi.org/10.1177/107769909607300314.

15 Charles R. Figley, "Compassion Fatigue: Psychotherapists' Chronic Lack of Self Care," *Journal of Clinical Psychology* 58, no. 11 (2002): 1433–41, https://doi.org/10.1002/jclp.10090; Carlton David Craig and Ginny Sprang, "Compassion Satisfaction, Compassion Fatigue, and Burnout in a National Sample of Trauma Treatment Therapists," *Anxiety, Stress, & Coping* 23, no. 3 (2010): 319–39, https://doi.org/10.1080/10615800903085818.

16 Kinnick, Krugman, and Cameron, "Compassion Fatigue."

17 David Conrad and Yvonne Kellar-Guenther, "Compassion Fatigue, Burnout, and Compassion Satisfaction among Colorado Child Protection Workers," *Child Abuse & Neglect* 30, no. 10 (2006): 1071–80, https://doi.org/10.1016/j.chiabu.2006.03.009.

18 Here a philosopher—and only a philosopher—might object that we don't actually need to feel compassion for anyone to do the right thing and help them whenever we can. We just need to help them. Fair enough. But then we're owed some other explanation for what will motivate this behavior that happens to line up with what compassion would move us to do, but doesn't fall prey to this same problem. It seems likely to us that any emotion is likely to be exhausted in the same way. But we'll return to this thought in the next section.

19 Anna Freud, *The Ego and the Mechanisms of Defence*, trans. Cecil Baines (New York: Routledge, 2018).

20 Plutarch, *Moralia*, 6:479.

21 Plutarch, 6:479–81.

22 Beth J. Seelig and Lisa S. Rosof, "Normal and Pathological Altruism," *Journal of the American Psychoanalytic Association* 49, no. 3 (2001): 953, https://doi.org/10.1177/00030651010490031901.

23 Seelig and Rosof, 953.

24 Barbara A. Oakley, Ariel Knafo, and Michael McGrath, "Pathological Altruism: An Introduction," in *Pathological Altruism*, ed. Barbara A. Oakley et al. (New York: Oxford University Press, 2011), 6.

25 Oakley, Knafo, and McGrath, 6.

26 Rachel Bachner-Melman and Barbara A. Oakley, "Giving 'Til It Hurts': Eating Disorders and Pathological Altruism," in *Bio-Psycho-Social Contributions to Understanding Eating Disorders*, ed. Yael Latzer and Daniel Stein (Switzerland: Springer, 2016), 91–103; Heinz Kohut, *The Analysis of the Self* (Chicago, IL: University of Chicago Press, 1971).

27 Indeed, for several accounts of people who seem to have lived in just this way, see Larissa MacFarquhar, *Strangers Drowning: Impossible Idealism, Drastic Choices, and the Urge to Help* (New York: Penguin, 2016).

4

1 Diane Coffey and Dean Spears, *Where India Goes: Abandoned Toilets, Stunted Development and the Costs of Caste* (Noida, Uttar Pradesh: HarperCollins India, 2017), 104.

2 www.teachforamerica.org/ [accessed 3/14/2022].

3 www.peacecorps.gov/volunteer/is-peace-corps-right-for-me/ [accessed 3/14/2022].

4　Due diligence reveals that (heavily diluted) bleach baths are a recommended treatment for eczema. See www.aad.org/public/diseases/eczema/childhood/treating/bleach-bath [accessed 5/28/2022].

5　See Coffey and Spears, *Where India Goes*, chap. 2.

6　https://mediaindia.eu/society/70066-open-defecation-free/ [accessed 8/13/2022].

7　Coffey and Spears, *Where India Goes*.

8　Interestingly, and in support of this claim, Coffey and Spears point out that the problem of open defecation and its consequences are less severe in areas of India with greater Muslim populations.

9　Aashish Gupta et al., "Revisiting Open Defecation: Evidence from a Panel Survey in Rural North India, 2014–18," *Economic & Political Weekly* 55, no. 21 (2020): 55–63.

10　This example is drawn from William MacAskill, *Doing Good Better: How Effective Altruism Can Help You Help Others, Do Work That Matters, and Make Smarter Choices about Giving Back* (Penguin Publishing Group, 2016), 1–5.

11　Sam Peltzman, "The Effects of Automobile Safety Regulation," *Journal of Political Economy* 83, no. 4 (1975): 677–725.

12　See, e.g., Christopher Garbacz, "Do Front-Seat Belt Laws Put Rear-Seat Passengers at Risk?," *Population Research and Policy Review* 11, no. 2 (1992): 157–68, https://doi.org/10.1007/BF00125536; Steven E. Rhoads, *The Economist's View of the World* (Cambridge: Cambridge University Press, 1985), 239; Alan Irwin, "Technical Expertise and Risk Conflict: An Institutional Study of the British Compulsory Seat Belt Debate," *Policy Sciences* 20, no. 4 (1987): 339–64, https://doi.org/10.1007/BF00135870; Robert Jervis, "Complexity and the Analysis of Political and Social Life," *Political Science Quarterly* 112, no. 4 (1997): 569–93, https://doi.org/10.2307/2657692.

13　David J. Houston, Lilliard E. Richardson, and Grant W. Neeley, "Legislating Traffic Safety: A Pooled Time Series Analysis," *Social Science Quarterly* 76, no. 2 (1995): 328–45; A. C. Harvey and J. Durbin, "The Effects of Seat Belt Legislation on British Road Casualties: A Case Study in Structural Time Series Modelling," *Journal of the Royal Statistical Society: Series A (General)* 149, no. 3 (1986): 187–210, https://doi.org/10.2307/2981553; David L. Ryan and Guy A. Bridgeman,

"Judging the Roles of Legislation, Education and Offsetting Behaviour in Seat Belt Use: A Survey and New Evidence from Alberta," *Canadian Public Policy / Analyse de Politiques* 18, no. 1 (1992): 27–46, https://doi.org/10.2307/3551553.

14 Christopher Garbacz, "Estimating Seat Belt Effectiveness with Seat Belt Usage Data from the Centers for Disease Control," *Economics Letters* 34, no. 1 (1990): 83–88, https://doi.org/10.1016/0165-1765(90)90186-5. We draw this survey of the literature from Jerry Gaus's thorough discussion in *The Open Society and Its Complexities* (New York: Oxford University Press, 2021), 189–91.

15 *Justice as Fairness: A Restatement* (Cambridge, Mass: Harvard University Press, 2001), 137.

16 https://ourworldindata.org/extreme-poverty#historical-poverty-around-the-world [accessed 8/16/2022].

17 https://ourworldindata.org/literacy#historical-change-in-literacy [accessed 8/16/2022].

18 https://ourworldindata.org/child-mortality#child-mortality-around-the-world-since-1800 [accessed 8/16/2022].

19 On the Great Divergence, see Angus Deaton, *The Great Escape: Health, Wealth, and the Origins of Inequality* (Princeton, NJ: Princeton University Press, 2013); Kenneth Pomeranz, *The Great Divergence: China, Europe, and the Making of the Modern World Economy* (Princeton, NJ: Princeton University Press, 2021). For a helpful discussion of its normative implications, see Dan Moller, "Justice and the Wealth of Nations," *Public Affairs Quarterly* 28, no. 2 (2014): 95–114.

20 Deirdre N. McCloskey, *If You're So Smart: The Narrative of Economic* Expertise (Chicago, IL: University of Chicago Press, 1990), 1.

21 Though we both like capitalism pretty well, we have expressed some mild reservations elsewhere. See Justin Tosi and Brandon Warmke, "Conservative Critiques," in *The Routledge Companion to Libertarianism*, ed. Matt Zwolinski and Benjamin Ferguson (London: Routledge, 2022), 579–92.

22 *An Inquiry Into the Nature and Causes of the Wealth of Nations*, ed. R. H. Campbell (Indianapolis, IN: Liberty Fund, 1982), sec. I.ii.2.

23 Fritz Heider, *The Psychology of Interpersonal Relations* (Mansfield Centre, CT: Martino Fine Books, 2015).

5

1 www.nytimes.com/interactive/2015/12/24/upshot/24up-family. html [accessed 8/25/22].

2 Malcolm Muggeridge, *The Infernal Grove: Chronicles of a Wasted Time: Number 2* (New York: William Morrow, 1974), 210.

3 Roy Pierce, *Contemporary French Political Thought* (Oxford, UK: Oxford University Press, 1966), 121.

4 Simone Weil, *The Need for Roots: Prelude to a Declaration of Duties Towards Mankind*, trans. Arthur Wills (London: Routledge, 2005), p. viii.

5 See Ronald Beiner, *Political Philosophy: What It Is and Why It Matters* (New York: Cambridge University Press, 2014), chap. 7.

6 Weil, *The Need for Roots*, 40.

7 For a recent review see Maria Lewicka, "Place Attachment: How Far Have We Come in the Last 40 Years?," *Journal of Environmental Psychology* 31, no. 3 (2011): 207–30, https://doi.org/10.1016/j.jenvp.2010.10.001. The scientific study of how humans relate to places that are meaningful to them remains a relatively young field.

8 Leila Scannell and Robert Gifford, "Defining Place Attachment: A Tripartite Organizing Framework," *Journal of Environmental Psychology* 30, no. 1 (2010): 1–10, https://doi.org/10.1016/j.jenvp.2009.09.006. Much of what we say here follows their model.

9 Yi-fu Tuan, *Topophilia: A Study of Environmental Perception, Attitudes, and Values* (New York: Columbia University Press, 1990).

10 One apparently robust finding, replicated across several countries, is that people experience higher levels of attachment to homes and cities than they do to their neighborhood. We will discuss the home in the next chapter. See Bernardo Hernández et al., "Place Attachment and Place Identity in Natives and Non-Natives," *Journal of Environmental Psychology* 27, no. 4 (2007): 310–19, https://doi.org/10.1016/j.jenvp.2007.06.003; M. Carmen Hidalgo and Bernardo Hernández, "Place Attachment: Conceptual and Empirical Questions," *Journal of Environmental Psychology* 21, no. 3 (2001): 273–81, https://doi.org/10.1006/jevp.2001.0221.

11 Tammy English et al., "Homesickness and Adjustment across the First Year of College: A Longitudinal Study," *Emotion* 17, no. 1 (2017): 1–5, https://doi.org/10.1037/emo0000235.

12 Homer, *The Odyssey*, trans. Robert Fagles (New York: Viking, 1996), 159.

13 Richard V. Francaviglia, "Xenia Rebuilds: Effects of Predisaster Conditioning on Postdisaster Redevelopment," *Journal of the American Institute of Planners* 44, no. 1 (1978): 13–24, https://doi.org/10.1080/01944367808976873.

14 Lewicka, "Place Attachment," 225.

15 Lewicka, 225. See also Robert Hay, "Sense of Place in Developmental Context," *Journal of Environmental Psychology* 18, no. 1 (1998): 5–29, https://doi.org/10.1006/jevp.1997.0060.

16 Lewicka, "Place Attachment."

17 Lewicka.

18 Harry F. Harlow, "The Development of Affectional Patterns in Infant Monkeys," in *Determinants of Infant Behaviour*, ed. B. M. Foss (Oxford, UK: Wiley, 1961), 75–88.

19 See, e.g., Mindy Thompson Fullilove, "Psychiatric Implications of Displacement: Contributions from the Psychology of Place," *American Journal of Psychiatry* 153, no. 12 (1996): 1516–23.

20 Roger T. Webb, Carsten B. Pedersen, and Pearl L. H. Mok, "Adverse Outcomes to Early Middle Age Linked with Childhood Residential Mobility," *American Journal of Preventive Medicine* 51, no. 3 (2016): 291–300, https://doi.org/10.1016/j.amepre.2016.04.011.

21 Hugh Hammond Bennett and William Ridgely Chapline, *Soil Erosion a National Menace* (Washington, DC: U.S. Department of Agriculture, 1928).

22 David Pimentel, "Soil Erosion: A Food and Environmental Threat," *Environment, Development and Sustainability* 8, no. 1 (2006): 119–37, https://doi.org/10.1007/s10668-005-1262-8.

23 See Sarah De Baets et al., "Micro-Scale Interactions between Arabidopsis Root Hairs and Soil Particles Influence Soil Erosion," *Communications Biology* 3, no. 1 (2020): 1–11, https://doi.org/10.1038/s42003-020-0886-4.

24 David Schmidtz, "The Institution of Property," *Social Philosophy and Policy* 11, no. 2 (1994): 48, https://doi.org/10.1017/S0265052500004428.

25 Wolfgang Streeck and Kathleen Ann Thelen, "Introduction," in *Beyond Continuity: Institutional Change in Advanced Political Economies*, ed. Wolfgang Streeck and Kathleen Ann Thelen (Oxford, UK: Oxford University Press, 2005), 9–11.

26 Douglass C. North, "Institutions," *Journal of Economic Perspectives* 5, no. 1 (1991): 97–112.

27 Of course, even large national-level associations are subject to erosion, too. Political scientist Theda Skocpol and her colleagues collected a list of 58 organizations that at some point from 1733 to 2004 included over 1 percent of the U.S. adult population as members. They found that 16 of these have ceased to exist—though in many cases this can clearly be attributed to the success of their mission, such as the American Anti-Slavery Society, which disbanded in 1870. Some readers will be relieved to hear that the Women's International Bowling Congress continued to enroll over 1 percent of the adult population at least as late as 2004. See Theda Skocpol, *Diminished Democracy: From Membership to Management in American Civic Life* (Norman, Oklahoma: University of Oklahoma Press, 2013), 26–28.

28 Thomas Cahill, *How the Irish Saved Civilization: The Untold Story of Ireland's Heroic Role from the Fall of Rome to the Rise of Medieval Europe* (New York: Doubleday, 1995).

29 https://forum.savingplaces.org/learn/fundamentals/preservation-law/local-laws [accessed 10/2/22].

30 www.cnn.com/2022/05/31/us/schools-after-mass-shootings-uvalde-texas/index.html [accessed 9/19/22].

31 Weil, *The Need for Roots*, 40.

32 Weil, 7.

33 Marc Fried, "Continuities and Discontinuities of Place," *Journal of Environmental Psychology* 20, no. 3 (2000): 193–205, https://doi.org/10.1006/jevp.1999.0154.

34 Edward Shils, *Tradition*, Reprint (Chicago, IL: University of Chicago Press, 2006), 2.

6

1 Philosophers David Jenkins and Kimberly Brownlee write of a "rich notion of a home which focuses on meeting our social needs including, specifically, our needs to belong and to have meaningful control over our social environment." "What a Home Does," *Law and Philosophy* 41, no. 4 (2022): 443, https://doi.org/10.1007/s10982-021-09414-w. This is the sense of home we have in mind here.

2 www.jchs.harvard.edu/research-areas/remodeling [accessed 10/17/2022].

3 www.usnews.com/education/best-colleges/articles/2017-08-31/ study-students-spent-59b-furnishing-their-college-dorms   [accessed 10/17/2022].

4 For a history of the more pedestrian aspects of the home, see Bill Bryson, *At Home: A Short History of Private Life*, Reprint (New York: Anchor, 2011).

5 www.cdc.gov/niosh/docs/99-101/default.html [accessed 10/31/2022].

6 www.apa.org/news/press/releases/stress/2016/coping-with-change.pdf [accessed 11/1/2022].

7 Kevin B. Smith, Matthew V. Hibbing, and John R. Hibbing, "Friends, Relatives, Sanity, and Health: The Costs of Politics," *PLOS ONE* 14, no. 9 (2019), https://doi.org/10.1371/journal.pone.0221870.

8 Of course, many employers are eager to invade this refuge. On this problem see Matthew Lister, "That's None of Your Business! On the Limits of Employer Control of Employee Behavior Outside of Working Hours," *Canadian Journal of Law & Jurisprudence* 35, no. 2 (2022): 405–26, https://doi.org/10.1017/cjlj.2022.6.

9 Thomas Nagel, "Concealment and Exposure," *Philosophy & Public Affairs* 27, no. 1 (1998): 3–30.

10 G.A. Cohen, *Why Not Socialism?* (Princeton, NJ: Princeton University Press, 2009), chap. 1.

11 Leon R. Kass, *The Hungry Soul: Eating and the Perfecting of Our Nature* (Chicago, IL: The University of Chicago Press, 1999), 107.

12 Christopher Lasch, *Haven in a Heartless World: The Family Besieged* (New York: W. W. Norton & Company, 1995), xxiv.

13 www.bgsu.edu/catalog/colleges-and-programs/college-of-education-and-human-development/tourism-hospitality-and-event-management.html [accessed 12/14/22].

14 https://undergrad.osu.edu/majors-and-academics/majors/detail/82 [accessed 12/14/22].

15 Our thinking about hospitality in this section is indebted to Kass, *The Hungry Soul*.

16 For background on Bedouin culture, we have been helped by Clinton Bailey, *Bedouin Culture in the Bible* (New Haven, CT: Yale University Press, 2018).

17 We quote here from Genesis 18:1–8. *Holy Bible: New International Version* (Zondervan Publishing House, 2005)

18 About 36 pounds, or 16 kilograms.

19 Hebrews 13:2. *Holy Bible: New International Version*.

20 Plato, *Laws*, trans. Benjamin Jowett, 3rd ed., vol. 5, The Dialogues of Plato (New York: Oxford University Press, 1892), 343.

21 Homer, *The Odyssey*, 81.

22 Homer, 87.

23 Henri J. M. Nouwen, *Reaching Out: The Three Movements of the Spiritual Life*, Reissue edition (Garden City, NY: Image, 1986), 66.

24 Though see John B. Bennett, "The Academy and Hospitality," *CrossCurrents* 50, no. 1/2 (2000): 23–35; John B. Bennett, *Academic Life: Hospitality, Ethics, and Spirituality* (Eugene, Oregon: Wipf and Stock Publishers, 2008); Aaron D. Cobb, *A Virtue-Based Defense of Perinatal Hospice* (New York: Routledge, 2019).

25 Nouwen, *Reaching Out*, 66.

26 Homer, *The Odyssey*, 321.

27 See Nouwen, *Reaching Out*, chap. 5; Bennett, "The Academy and Hospitality"; Bennett, *Academic Life*, chap. 3.

28 Plato, *Laws*, 5:21.

29 Some readers will notice that we haven't discussed the family in relation to the home. For those interested in the benefits of the home for raising a family, see Brandon Warmke, "Changing the World Starts at Home," *Georgetown Journal of Law & Public Policy*, forthcoming.

30 For more on neighborliness, and the importance of loving particular others, not abstract others, see David McPherson, *The Virtues of Limits* (New York: Oxford University Press, 2022).

7

1 Christopher R. Long and James R. Averill, "Solitude: An Exploration of Benefits of Being Alone," *Journal for the Theory of Social Behaviour* 33, no. 1 (2003): 21–44, https://doi.org/10.1111/1468-5914.00204. They are summarizing Peter Suedfeld, "Aloneness as a Healing Experience," in *Loneliness: A Sourcebook of Current Theory, Research and Therapy*, ed. Letitia Anne Peplau and Daniel Perlman (New York: Wiley & Sons, 1982), 54–67.

2 John Stuart Mill, *Principles of Political Economy, Part II*, ed. John M. Robson, vol. 3, Collected Works of John Stuart Mill (Toronto: University of Toronto Press, 1965), 756.

3 For perhaps the most detailed modern philosophical treatment of solitude, see Philip Koch, *Solitude: A Philosophical Encounter* (Chicago, IL: Open Court Publishing Company, 1994). Much of what we say here about solitude is indebted to that discussion. See also Anthony Storr, *Solitude: A Return to the Self*, Reissue edition (New York: Free Press, 2005). See also Michel de Montaigne's essay "On Solitude" in *The Complete Works* (New York: Everyman's Library, 2003), 211–22.

4 We owe the terminology in this paragraph to David Vincent, *A History of Solitude* (Cambridge, UK: Polity, 2020), 22–23.

5 Vincent calls this physical distance marked by social connectedness "networked solitude."

6 See Koch, *Solitude*, 31–34; Tom Roberts and Joel Krueger, "Loneliness and the Emotional Experience of Absence," *The Southern Journal of Philosophy* 59, no. 2 (2021): 185–204, https://doi.org/10.1111/sjp.12387.

7 Long and Averill, "Solitude," 37.

8 For a review see Richard Schacht, *Alienation*, 1st ed. (London: Psychology Press, 1970), https://doi.org/10.4324/9781315712703.

9 Interested readers may find more to think about in Storr, *Solitude*; Koch, *Solitude*; Stephen Batchelor, *The Art of Solitude* (New Haven, CT: Yale University Press, 2020), https://doi.org/10.2307/j.ctvwcjf38.

10 Robert Nisbet, *The Quest for Community: A Study in the Ethics of Order & Freedom* (San Francisco, CA: Intercollegiate Studies Institute, 1990).

11 See Josef Pieper, *Leisure: The Basis of Culture* (Indianapolis, IN: Liberty Fund, 1999).

12 See Mark R. Leary and Robin M. Kowalski, "Impression Management: A Literature Review and Two-Component Model," *Psychological Bulletin* 107, no. 1 (1990): 34–47, https://doi.org/10.1037/0033-2909.107.1.34. We discuss the way impression management specifically affects our contributions to public discourse in Tosi and Warmke, *Grandstanding.*

13 Long and Averill, "Solitude," 37.

14 Long and Averill, 38. For more on social status hierarchies, see Gerben A. van Kleef and Joey T. Cheng, "Power, Status, and Hierarchy: Current Trends and Future Challenges," *Current Opinion in Psychology*, Power, Status and Hierarchy, 33 (2020): iv–xiii, https://doi.org/10.1016/j.copsyc.2020.03.011.

15 John Clare, *The Village Minstrel: And Other Poems* (London: Taylor & Hessey, 1821), 206.

16 Claudia Hammond and Gemma Lewis, "The Rest Test: Preliminary Findings from a Large-Scale International Survey on Rest," in *The Restless Compendium: Interdisciplinary Investigations of Rest and Its Opposites*, ed. Felicity Callard, Kimberley Staines, and James Wilkes (Basingstoke, UK: Palgrave Macmillan, 2016), 59–67, https://doi.org/10.1007/978-3-319-45264-7_8.

17 Thuy-vy T. Nguyen, Richard M. Ryan, and Edward L. Deci, "Solitude as an Approach to Affective Self-Regulation," *Personality and Social Psychology Bulletin* 44, no. 1 (January 1, 2018): 15, https://doi.org/10.1177/0146167217733073.

18 See, for example, Koch, *Solitude*, 104–9.

19 Long and Averill, "Solitude," 23.

20 William Hazlitt, *Table-Talk: Essays on Men and Manners* (London: Lutheran Publication Society, 1869), 249–51. Quoted in Koch, *Solitude*, 104.

21 Matthew Arnold, *Culture & Anarchy: An Essay in Political and Social Criticism; and Friendship's Garland* (New York: Macmillan, 1896), 344.

22 Here we are indebted to the discussion of Mill's views on solitude in Guy Paltieli, "Mill's Closet: J.S. Mill on Solitude and the Imperfect Democracy," *History of European Ideas* 45, no. 1 (2019): 47–63, https://doi.org/10.1080/01916599.2018.1527558.

23 John Stuart Mill, *The Earlier Letters of John Stuart Mill: 1812–1848, Part I*, ed. Francis E. Mineka, vol. 12, Collected Works of John Stuart Mill (Toronto: University of Toronto Press, 1963), 153.

24 John Stuart Mill, *Autobiography and Literary Essays*, ed. John M. Robson and Jack Stillinger, vol. 1, Collected Works of John Stuart Mill (Toronto: University of Toronto Press, 1981), 338.

25 John Stuart Mill, *The Later Letters of John Stuart Mill: 1849–1873, Part II*, ed. Francis E. Mineka and Dwight N. Lindley, vol. 15, Collected Works of John Stuart Mill (Toronto: University of Toronto Press, 1972), 855n2.

26 Irving L. Janis, *Groupthink: Psychological Studies of Policy Decisions and Fiascoes*, 2nd ed. (Boston, MA: Cengage Learning, 1982); Solomon E. Asch, "Studies of Independence and Conformity: A Minority of One against a Unanimous Majority," *Psychological Monographs: General and Applied* 70, no. 9 (1956): 1–70.

27 Mill, *The Later Letters of John Stuart Mill: 1849–1873, Part II*, 15:548.

28 Solitude is sometimes claimed to be an important catalyst for creativity. See Storr, *Solitude*; Koch, *Solitude*. For empirical discussion, see Long and Averill, "Solitude."

29 Denis Diderot, *Encyclopédie, ou, Dictionnaire raisonné des sciences, des arts et des métiers*, vol. 15 (Paris: Chez Briasson, 1765), 324. Quoted in Vincent, *A History of Solitude*, 4.

30 Christian Miller, *The Character Gap: How Good Are We?* (Oxford, UK: Oxford University Press, 2017).

31 In conversation with Peter Whittle: www.youtube.com/watch?v=pz-fPOjXqL4 [accessed 12/7/22].

32 Epictetus, *Discourses and Selected Writings*, trans. Robert Dobbin (London: Penguin Classics, 2008), 230.

EPILOGUE

1 David Foster Wallace, *This Is Water: Some Thoughts, Delivered on a Significant Occasion, about Living a Compassionate Life* (New York: Little, Brown & Company, 2009), 3–4.

2 Wallace, 8–10.

References

Alston, Richard M., J. R. Kearl, and Michael B. Vaughan. "Is There a Consensus Among Economists in the 1990's?" *The American Economic Review* 82, no. 2 (1992): 203–9.

Anthis, Jacy Reese, and Eze Paez. "Moral Circle Expansion: A Promising Strategy to Impact the Far Future." *Futures* 130 (2021): 102756. https://doi.org/10.1016/j.futures.2021.102756.

Aristotle. *The Complete Works of Aristotle: The Revised Oxford Translation*. Edited by Jonathan Barnes. Revised Edition. Vol. 2. Princeton, N.J: Princeton University Press, 1984.

Arnold, Matthew. *Culture & Anarchy: An Essay in Political and Social Criticism; and Friendship's Garland*. New York: Macmillan, 1896.

Asch, Solomon E. "Studies of Independence and Conformity: A Minority of One against a Unanimous Majority." *Psychological Monographs: General and Applied* 70, no. 9 (1956): 1–70.

Bachner-Melman, Rachel, and Barbara A. Oakley. "Giving 'Til It Hurts': Eating Disorders and Pathological Altruism." In *Bio-Psycho-Social Contributions to Understanding Eating Disorders*, edited by Yael Latzer and Daniel Stein, 91–103. Switzerland: Springer, 2016.

Bailey, Clinton. *Bedouin Culture in the Bible*. New Haven, CT: Yale University Press, 2018.

Ballantyne, Nathan. "Epistemic Trespassing." *Mind* 128, no. 510 (2019): 367–95. https://doi.org/10.1093/mind/fzx042.

Batchelor, Stephen. *The Art of Solitude*. New Haven, CT: Yale University Press, 2020. https://doi.org/10.2307/j.ctvwcjf38.

Beiner, Ronald. *Political Philosophy: What It Is and Why It Matters*. New York: Cambridge University Press, 2014.

Bennett, Hugh Hammond, and William Ridgely Chapline. *Soil Erosion a National Menace*. Washington, DC: U.S. Department of Agriculture, 1928.

Bennett, John B. *Academic Life: Hospitality, Ethics, and Spirituality*. Eugene, OR: Wipf and Stock Publishers, 2008.

———. "The Academy and Hospitality." *CrossCurrents* 50, no. 1/2 (2000): 23–35.

Bicknell, Jeanette. "Self-Righteousness as a Moral Problem." *The Journal of Value Inquiry* 44, no. 4 (2010): 477–87. https://doi.org/10.1007/s10790-010-9247-8.

Block, Walter, and Michael Walker. "Entropy in the Canadian Economics Profession: Sampling Consensus on the Major Issues." *Canadian Public Policy / Analyse de Politiques* 14, no. 2 (1988): 137–50. https://doi.org/10.2307/3550573.

Bratanova, Boyka, Steve Loughnan, and Birgitta Gatersleben. "The Moral Circle as a Common Motivational Cause of Cross-Situational pro-Environmentalism." *European Journal of Social Psychology* 42, no. 5 (2012): 539–45. https://doi.org/10.1002/ejsp.1871.

Brown, Jeannine K. "Just a Busybody? A Look at the Greco-Roman Topos of Meddling for Defining Hebrew in 1 Peter 4:15." *Journal of Biblical Literature* 125, no. 3 (2006): 549–68. https://doi.org/10.2307/27638379.

Bryson, Bill. *At Home: A Short History of Private Life*. Reprint. New York: Anchor, 2011.

Cahill, Thomas. *How the Irish Saved Civilization: The Untold Story of Ireland's Heroic Role from the Fall of Rome to the Rise of Medieval Europe*. New York: Doubleday, 1995.

Clare, John. *The Village Minstrel: And Other Poems*. London: Taylor & Hessey, 1821.

Cobb, Aaron D. *A Virtue-Based Defense of Perinatal Hospice*. New York: Routledge, 2019.

Coffey, Diane, and Dean Spears. *Where India Goes: Abandoned Toilets, Stunted Development and the Costs of Caste*. Noida, Uttar Pradesh: HarperCollins India, 2017.

Cohen, G.A. *Why Not Socialism?* Princeton, NJ: Princeton University Press, 2009.

Conrad, David, and Yvonne Kellar-Guenther. "Compassion Fatigue, Burnout, and Compassion Satisfaction among Colorado Child Protection Workers." *Child Abuse & Neglect* 30, no. 10 (2006): 1071–80. https://doi.org/10.1016/j.chiabu.2006.03.009.

Craig, Carlton David, and Ginny Sprang. "Compassion Satisfaction, Compassion Fatigue, and Burnout in a National Sample of Trauma Treatment Therapists." *Anxiety, Stress, & Coping* 23, no. 3 (2010): 319–39. https://doi.org/10.1080/10615800903085818.

De Baets, Sarah, Thomas D. G. Denbigh, Kevin M. Smyth, Bethany M. Eldridge, Laura Weldon, Benjamin Higgins, Antoni Matyjaszkiewicz, et al. "Micro-Scale Interactions between Arabidopsis Root Hairs and Soil Particles Influence Soil Erosion." *Communications Biology* 3, no. 1 (2020): 1–11. https://doi.org/10.1038/s42003-020-0886-4.

Deaton, Angus. *The Great Escape: Health, Wealth, and the Origins of Inequality.* Princeton, NJ: Princeton University Press, 2013.

Dickens, Charles. *A Christmas Carol and Other Stories.* New York: Modern Library, 2001.

Dickinson, David L., and David Masclet. "Emotion Venting and Punishment in Public Good Experiments." *Journal of Public Economics* 122 (February 1, 2015): 55–67. https://doi.org/10.1016/j.jpubeco.2014.10.008.

Diderot, Denis. *Encyclopédie, ou, Dictionnaire raisonné des sciences, des arts et des métiers.* Vol. 15. Paris: Chez Briasson, 1765.

Driver, Julia. "Hyperactive Ethics." *The Philosophical Quarterly* 44, no. 174 (1994): 9–25. https://doi.org/10.2307/2220144.

———. "Moralism." *Journal of Applied Philosophy* 22, no. 2 (2005): 137–51. https://doi.org/10.1111/j.1468-5930.2005.00298.x.

English, Tammy, Jordan Davis, Melissa Wei, and James J. Gross. "Homesickness and Adjustment across the First Year of College: A Longitudinal Study." *Emotion* 17, no. 1 (2017): 1–5. https://doi.org/10.1037/emo0000235.

Epictetus. *Discourses and Selected Writings.* Translated by Robert Dobbin. London: Penguin Classics, 2008.

———. *Discourses, Books 3–4. Fragments. The Encheiridion.* Translated by W. A. Oldfather. Loeb Classical Library 218. Cambridge, MA: Harvard University Press, 1928.

Epstein, Seymour. "Expectancy and Magnitude of Reaction to a Noxious UCS." *Psychophysiology* 10, no. 1 (1973): 100–107. https://doi.org/10.1111/j.1469-8986.1973.tb01091.x.

Figley, Charles R. "Compassion Fatigue as Secondary Traumatic Stress Disorder: An Overview." In *Compassion Fatigue: Coping with Secondary Stress Disorder in Those Who Treat the Traumatised,* edited by Charles R. Figley. Bristol, UK: Brunner/Mazel, 1995.

———. "Compassion Fatigue: Psychotherapists' Chronic Lack of Self Care." *Journal of Clinical Psychology* 58, no. 11 (2002): 1433–41. https://doi.org/10.1002/jclp.10090.

Francaviglia, Richard V. "Xenia Rebuilds: Effects of Predisaster Conditioning on Postdisaster Redevelopment." *Journal of the American Institute of Planners* 44, no. 1 (1978): 13–24. https://doi.org/10.1080/01944367808976873.

Freud, Anna. *The Ego and the Mechanisms of Defence.* Translated by Cecil Baines. New York: Routledge, 2018.

Fried, Marc. "Continuities and Discontinuities of Place." *Journal of Environmental Psychology* 20, no. 3 (2000): 193–205. https://doi.org/10.1006/jevp.1999.0154.

Frijda, Nico H. *The Laws of Emotion.* Mahwah, NJ: Psychology Press, 2006.

Fritz, Kyle G., and Daniel J. Miller. "A Standing Asymmetry between Blame and Forgiveness." *Ethics* 132, no. 4 (2022): 759–86. https://doi.org/10.1086/719511.

Fullilove, Mindy Thompson. "Psychiatric Implications of Displacement: Contributions from the Psychology of Place." *American Journal of Psychiatry* 153, no. 12 (1996): 1516–23.

Fullinwider, Robert K. "On Moralism." *Journal of Applied Philosophy* 22, no. 2 (2005): 105–20.

Garbacz, Christopher. "Do Front-Seat Belt Laws Put Rear-Seat Passengers at Risk?" *Population Research and Policy Review* 11, no. 2 (1992): 157–68. https://doi.org/10.1007/BF00125536.

———. "Estimating Seat Belt Effectiveness with Seat Belt Usage Data from the Centers for Disease Control." *Economics Letters* 34, no. 1 (1990): 83–88. https://doi.org/10.1016/0165-1765(90)90186-5.

Gaus, Gerald. "On the Difficult Virtue of Minding One's Own Business: Towards the Political Rehabilitation of Ebenezer Scrooge." *The Philosopher: A Magazine for Free Spirits* 5 (1997): 24–28.

———. *The Open Society and Its Complexities.* New York: Oxford University Press, 2021.

———. *The Order of Public Reason: A Theory of Freedom and Morality in a Diverse and Bounded World.* New York: Cambridge University Press, 2011.

Gupta, Aashish, Nidhi Khalid, Devashish Deshpande, Payal Hathi, Avani Kapur, Nikhil Srivastav, Sangita Vyas, Dean Spears, and Diane Coffey. "Revisiting Open Defecation: Evidence from a Panel Survey in Rural North India, 2014–18." *Economic & Political Weekly* 55, no. 21 (2020): 55–63.

Hammond, Claudia, and Gemma Lewis. "The Rest Test: Preliminary Findings from a Large-Scale International Survey on Rest." In *The Restless Compendium: Interdisciplinary Investigations of Rest and Its Opposites*, edited by Felicity Callard, Kimberley Staines, and James Wilkes, 59–67. Basingstoke, UK: Palgrave Macmillan, 2016. https://doi.org/10.1007/978-3-319-45264-7_8.

Harlow, Harry F. "The Development of Affectional Patterns in Infant Monkeys." In *Determinants of Infant Behaviour*, edited by B.M. Foss, 75–88. Oxford, UK: Wiley, 1961.

Harvey, A. C., and J. Durbin. "The Effects of Seat Belt Legislation on British Road Casualties: A Case Study in Structural Time Series Modelling." *Journal of the Royal Statistical Society: Series A (General)* 149, no. 3 (1986): 187–210. https://doi.org/10.2307/2981553.

Hay, Robert. "Sense of Place in Developmental Context." *Journal of Environmental Psychology* 18, no. 1 (1998): 5–29. https://doi.org/10.1006/jevp.1997.0060.

Hazlitt, William. *Table-Talk: Essays on Men and Manners.* London: Lutheran Publication Society, 1869.

Heider, Fritz. *The Psychology of Interpersonal Relations.* Mansfield Centre, CT: Martino Fine Books, 2015.

Hernández, Bernardo, M. Carmen Hidalgo, M. Esther Salazar-Laplace, and Stephany Hess. "Place Attachment and Place Identity in Natives and Non-Natives." *Journal of Environmental Psychology* 27, no. 4 (2007): 310–19. https://doi.org/10.1016/j.jenvp.2007.06.003.

Hidalgo, M. Carmen, and Bernardo Hernández. "Place Attachment: Conceptual and Empirical Questions." *Journal of Environmental Psychology* 21, no. 3 (2001): 273–81. https://doi.org/10.1006/jevp.2001.0221.

Holy Bible: New International Version. Zondervan Publishing House, 2005.

Homer. *The Odyssey.* Translated by Robert Fagles. New York: Viking, 1996.

Houston, David J., Lilliard E. Richardson, and Grant W. Neeley. "Legislating Traffic Safety: A Pooled Time Series Analysis." *Social Science Quarterly* 76, no. 2 (1995): 328–45.

Irwin, Alan. "Technical Expertise and Risk Conflict: An Institutional Study of the British Compulsory Seat Belt Debate." *Policy Sciences* 20, no. 4 (1987): 339–64. https://doi.org/10.1007/BF00135870.

Janis, Irving L. *Groupthink: Psychological Studies of Policy Decisions and Fiascoes.* 2nd ed. Boston, MA: Cengage Learning, 1982.

Jenkins, David, and Kimberley Brownlee. "What a Home Does." *Law and Philosophy* 41, no. 4 (2022): 441–68. https://doi.org/10.1007/s10982-021-09414-w.

Jervis, Robert. "Complexity and the Analysis of Political and Social Life." *Political Science Quarterly* 112, no. 4 (1997): 569–93. https://doi.org/10.2307/2657692.

Kass, Leon R. *The Hungry Soul: Eating and the Perfecting of Our Nature.* Chicago, IL: The University of Chicago Press, 1999.

Kennedy, Jessica, and Maurice E. Schweitzer. "Holding People Responsible for Ethical Violations: The Surprising Benefits of Accusing Others."

Academy of Management Proceedings 2015, no. 1 (2015): 112–58. https://doi.org/10.5465/ambpp.2015.11258abstract.

Kinnick, Katherine N., Dean M. Krugman, and Glen T. Cameron. "Compassion Fatigue: Communication and Burnout toward Social Problems." *Journalism & Mass Communication Quarterly* 73, no. 3 (1996): 687–707. https://doi.org/10.1177/107769909607300314.

Kleef, Gerben A van, and Joey T Cheng. "Power, Status, and Hierarchy: Current Trends and Future Challenges." *Current Opinion in Psychology*, Power, Status and Hierarchy, 33 (2020): iv–xiii. https://doi.org/10.1016/j.copsyc.2020.03.011.

Koch, Philip. *Solitude: A Philosophical Encounter*. Chicago, IL: Open Court Publishing Company, 1994.

Kohut, Heinz. *The Analysis of the Self*. Chicago, IL: University of Chicago Press, 1971.

Laham, Simon M. "Expanding the Moral Circle: Inclusion and Exclusion Mindsets and the Circle of Moral Regard." *Journal of Experimental Social Psychology* 45, no. 1 (2009): 250–53. https://doi.org/10.1016/j.jesp.2008.08.012.

Lasch, Christopher. *Haven in a Heartless World: The Family Besieged*. New York: W. W. Norton & Company, 1995.

Leary, Mark R., and Robin M. Kowalski. "Impression Management: A Literature Review and Two-Component Model." *Psychological Bulletin* 107, no. 1 (1990): 34–47. https://doi.org/10.1037/0033-2909.107.1.34.

Lewicka, Maria. "Place Attachment: How Far Have We Come in the Last 40 Years?" *Journal of Environmental Psychology* 31, no. 3 (2011): 207–30. https://doi.org/10.1016/j.jenvp.2010.10.001.

Lewis, Sinclair. *It Can't Happen Here*. Reprint edition. New York: Signet, 2014.

Lister, Matthew. "That's None of Your Business! On the Limits of Employer Control of Employee Behavior Outside of Working Hours." *Canadian Journal of Law & Jurisprudence* 35, no. 2 (2022): 405–26. https://doi.org/10.1017/cjlj.2022.6.

Long, Christopher R., and James R. Averill. "Solitude: An Exploration of Benefits of Being Alone." *Journal for the Theory of Social Behaviour* 33, no. 1 (2003): 21–44. https://doi.org/10.1111/1468-5914.00204.

MacAskill, William. *Doing Good Better: How Effective Altruism Can Help You Help Others, Do Work That Matters, and Make Smarter Choices about Giving Back*. New York: Penguin Publishing Group, 2016.

MacFarquhar, Larissa. *Strangers Drowning: Impossible Idealism, Drastic Choices, and the Urge to Help*. New York: Penguin, 2016.

McCloskey, Deirdre N. *If You're So Smart: The Narrative of Economic Expertise*. Chicago, IL: University of Chicago Press, 1990.

McPherson, David. *The Virtues of Limits*. New York: Oxford University Press, 2022.

McSweeney, Frances K., and Samantha Swindell. "General-Process Theories of Motivation Revisited: The Role of Habituation." *Psychological Bulletin* 125, no. 4 (1999): 437.

Mill, John Stuart. *Autobiography and Literary Essays*. Edited by John M. Robson and Jack Stillinger. Vol. 1. 33 vols. Collected Works of John Stuart Mill. Toronto: University of Toronto Press, 1981.

———. *Essays On Ethics, Religion And Society*. Indianapolis, IN: Liberty Fund Inc., 2006.

———. *On Liberty and Other Writings*. Cambridge, UK: Cambridge University Press, 1989.

———. *Principles of Political Economy, Part II*. Edited by John M. Robson. Vol. 3. 33 vols. Collected Works of John Stuart Mill. Toronto: University of Toronto Press, 1965.

———. *The Earlier Letters of John Stuart Mill: 1812–1848, Part I*. Edited by Francis E. Mineka. Vol. 12. 33 vols. Collected Works of John Stuart Mill. Toronto: University of Toronto Press, 1963.

———. *The Later Letters of John Stuart Mill: 1849–1873, Part II*. Edited by Francis E. Mineka and Dwight N. Lindley. Vol. 15. 33 vols. Collected Works of John Stuart Mill. Toronto: University of Toronto Press, 1972.

Miller, Christian. *The Character Gap: How Good Are We?* Oxford, UK: Oxford University Press, 2017.

Moller, Dan. "Justice and the Wealth of Nations." *Public Affairs Quarterly* 28, no. 2 (2014): 95–114.

Montaigne, Michel de. *The Complete Works*. New York: Everyman's Library, 2003.

Muggeridge, Malcolm. *The Infernal Grove: Chronicles of a Wasted Time: Number 2*. New York: William Morrow, 1974.

Nagel, Thomas. "Concealment and Exposure." *Philosophy & Public Affairs* 27, no. 1 (1998): 3–30.

Nguyen, Thuy-vy T., Richard M. Ryan, and Edward L. Deci. "Solitude as an Approach to Affective Self-Regulation." *Personality and Social Psychology Bulletin* 44, no. 1 (January 1, 2018): 92–106. https://doi.org/10.1177/0146167217733073.

Nietzsche, Friedrich. *Thus Spoke Zarathustra: A Book for All and None*. Translated by Walter Kaufmann. New York: Modern Library, 1995.

Nisbet, Robert. *The Quest for Community: A Study in the Ethics of Order & Freedom*. San Francisco, CA: Intercollegiate Studies Institute, 1990.

North, Douglass C. "Institutions." *Journal of Economic Perspectives* 5, no. 1 (1991): 97–112.

Nouwen, Henri J. M. *Reaching Out: The Three Movements of the Spiritual Life*. Reissue edition. Garden City, NY: Image, 1986.

Nozick, Robert. *Anarchy, State, and Utopia*. New York: Basic Books, 1974.

Oakley, Barbara A., Ariel Knafo, and Michael McGrath. "Pathological Altruism: An Introduction." In *Pathological Altruism*, edited by Barbara A. Oakley, Ariel Knafo, Guruprasad Madhavan, and David Sloan Wilson, 3–9. New York: Oxford University Press, 2011.

Paltieli, Guy. "Mill's Closet: J.S. Mill on Solitude and the Imperfect Democracy." *History of European Ideas* 45, no. 1 (2019): 47–63. https://doi.org/10.1080/01916599.2018.1527558.

Peltzman, Sam. "The Effects of Automobile Safety Regulation." *Journal of Political Economy* 83, no. 4 (1975): 677–725.

Pieper, Josef. *Leisure: The Basis of Culture*. Indianapolis, IN: Liberty Fund, 1999.

Pierce, Roy. *Contemporary French Political Thought*. Oxford, UK: Oxford University Press, 1966.

Pimentel, David. "Soil Erosion: A Food and Environmental Threat." *Environment, Development and Sustainability* 8, no. 1 (2006): 119–37. https://doi.org/10.1007/s10668-005-1262-8.

Plato. *Laws*. Translated by Benjamin Jowett. 3rd ed. Vol. 5. The Dialogues of Plato. New York: Oxford University Press, 1892.

Plutarch. *Moralia*. Translated by William Clark Helmbold. Vol. 6. 16 vols. Loeb Classical Library 337. Cambridge, MA: Harvard University Press, 1939.

Pomeranz, Kenneth. *The Great Divergence: China, Europe, and the Making of the Modern World Economy*. Princeton: Princeton University Press, 2021.

Rawls, John. *Justice as Fairness: A Restatement*. Cambridge, MA: Harvard University Press, 2001.

Reed II, Americus, and Karl F. Aquino. "Moral Identity and the Expanding Circle of Moral Regard toward Out-Groups." *Journal of Personality and Social Psychology* 84 (2003): 1270–86. https://doi.org/10.1037/0022-3514.84.6.1270.

Rhoads, Steven E. *The Economist's View of the World*. Cambridge: Cambridge University Press, 1985.

Roberts, Tom, and Joel Krueger. "Loneliness and the Emotional Experience of Absence." *The Southern Journal of Philosophy* 59, no. 2 (2021): 185–204. https://doi.org/10.1111/sjp.12387.

Ross, David. *The Right and the Good*. New York: Oxford University Press, 2002.

Ryan, David L., and Guy A. Bridgeman. "Judging the Roles of Legislation, Education and Offsetting Behaviour in Seat Belt Use: A Survey and New Evidence from Alberta." *Canadian Public Policy / Analyse de Politiques* 18, no. 1 (1992): 27–46. https://doi.org/10.2307/3551553.

Scannell, Leila, and Robert Gifford. "Defining Place Attachment: A Tripartite Organizing Framework." *Journal of Environmental Psychology* 30, no. 1 (2010): 1–10. https://doi.org/10.1016/j.jenvp.2009.09.006.

Schacht, Richard. *Alienation*. 1st ed. London: Psychology Press, 1970. https://doi.org/10.4324/9781315712703.

Schmidtz, David. "The Institution of Property." *Social Philosophy and Policy* 11, no. 2 (1994): 42–62. https://doi.org/10.1017/S0265052500004428.

Seelig, Beth J., and Lisa S. Rosof. "Normal and Pathological Altruism." *Journal of the American Psychoanalytic Association* 49, no. 3 (2001): 933–59. https://doi.org/10.1177/00030651010490031901.

Shils, Edward. *Tradition*. Reprint. Chicago, IL: University of Chicago Press, 2006.

Singer, Peter. "Famine, Affluence, and Morality." *Philosophy & Public Affairs* 1, no. 3 (1972): 229–43.

———. *The Expanding Circle: Ethics, Evolution, and Moral Progress*. Revised. Princeton, NJ: Princeton University Press, 2011.

Skocpol, Theda. *Diminished Democracy: From Membership to Management in American Civic Life*. Norman, OK: University of Oklahoma Press, 2013.

Smith, Adam. *An Inquiry Into the Nature and Causes of the Wealth of Nations*. Edited by R. H. Campbell. Indianapolis, IN: Liberty Fund, 1982.

Smith, Kevin B., Matthew V. Hibbing, and John R. Hibbing. "Friends, Relatives, Sanity, and Health: The Costs of Politics." *PLOS ONE* 14, no. 9 (2019). https://doi.org/10.1371/journal.pone.0221870.

Storr, Anthony. *Solitude: A Return to the Self*. Reissue edition. New York: Free Press, 2005.

Strawson, P. F. "Social Morality and Individual Ideal." *Philosophy* 36, no. 136 (1961): 1–17.

Streeck, Wolfgang, and Kathleen Ann Thelen. "Introduction." In *Beyond Continuity: Institutional Change in Advanced Political Economies*, edited by

Wolfgang Streeck and Kathleen Ann Thelen, 1–39. Oxford, UK: Oxford University Press, 2005.

Suedfeld, Peter. "Aloneness as a Healing Experience." In *Loneliness: A Sourcebook of Current Theory, Research and Therapy*, edited by Letitia Anne Peplau and Daniel Perlman, 54–67. New York: Wiley & Sons, 1982.

Taylor, Thomas, trans. *Political Fragments of Archytas, Charondas, Zaleucus, and Other Ancient Pythagoreans, Preserved by Stobaeus, and Also, Ethical Fragments of Hierocles.* Walworth, UK: Printed by C. Whittingham for the translator, 1822.

Theophrastus. *The Characters of Theophrastus.* Translated by Isaac Taylor. London: A.J. Valpy, 1831.

Thucydides. *History of the Peloponnesian War.* Translated by Rex Warner. Revised Edition. Harmondsworth, UK: Penguin Classics, 1972.

Todd, Patrick. "A Unified Account of the Moral Standing to Blame." *Noûs* 53, no. 2 (2019): 347–74. https://doi.org/10.1111/nous.12215.

Tosi, Justin, and Brandon Warmke. "Conservative Critiques." In *The Routledge Companion to Libertarianism*, edited by Matt Zwolinski and Benjamin Ferguson, 579–92. London: Routledge, 2022.

———. *Grandstanding: The Use and Abuse of Moral Talk.* New York: Oxford University Press, 2020.

Tuan, Yi-fu. *Topophilia: A Study of Environmental Perception, Attitudes, and Values.* New York: Columbia University Press, 1990.

Vincent, David. *A History of Solitude.* Cambridge, UK: Polity, 2020.

Wallace, David Foster. *This Is Water: Some Thoughts, Delivered on a Significant Occasion, about Living a Compassionate Life.* New York: Little, Brown & Company, 2009.

Warmke, Brandon. "Changing the World Starts at Home." *Georgetown Journal of Law & Public Policy*, forthcoming.

Webb, Roger T., Carsten B. Pedersen, and Pearl L. H. Mok. "Adverse Outcomes to Early Middle Age Linked with Childhood Residential Mobility." *American Journal of Preventive Medicine* 51, no. 3 (2016): 291–300. https://doi.org/10.1016/j.amepre.2016.04.011.

Weil, Simone. *The Need for Roots: Prelude to a Declaration of Duties Towards Mankind.* Translated by Arthur Wills. London: Routledge, 2005.

Williams, Bernard. *Ethics and the Limits of Philosophy.* Cambridge, MA: Harvard University Press, 1986.

Index

Made in United States
Cleveland, OH
28 January 2025